The Winning Mind Set™

Unleash the Power of Your Mind

Praise for *The Winning Mind Set*™ techniques

"Thank you for giving me advice on how to be a better athlete mentally and physically. With the advice and exercises you showed me, I have improved my performance out on the water."
Clinton Bolton
Professional Kitesurfer
2005 US Kiteboarding Champion

"Hands down one of the best books I have read this year. A crowning achievement in the realm of human potential and development, this book is sure to open the eyes of many and unleash the powers within."
Anthony Iglesias
Professional Musician/Performer

"I found The Winning Mind Set personally rewarding because it pushed my limits and perceptions of myself. You're right, the mind always moves in the direction of your dominant thoughts"
Doug Weinburg

"The Winning Mind Set has made a monumental difference in my level of self-confidence and consequently helped me in many areas of my life. I have stopped smoking, lost 34 lbs., and made a conscious daily effort to stay organized and on task on a more committed level. I used to make excuses to myself as to why I couldn't accomplish the things that I needed to in order to succeed in my life, now I believe I can accomplish anything I prepare myself to. I'm very excited to see what my future will bring. Thank you."
Jonathon Comstock
Business Owner and Entrepreneur

"The positive benefits I receive from "The Winning Mind Set" are priceless. When I first signed up to receive the newsletter it was for competition in the Kiteboarding World Cup Tour, to get the competitive mental edge that I believe is crucial to winning. What I have found over the years is that the same principles that help athletes win at the competitions have helped me incredibly with my professional and personal life."
Laurel Eastman
Professional Business Woman

"I wholeheartedly endorse the techniques, strategies and philosophies in The Winning Mind Set. I believe that anyone who applies what they learn will see significant measurable increases in their results. My confidence comes from first-hand experience. Speaking of my business, it has grown significantly. As you know, I've been a top producer in direct marketing for several years. In the last six months alone, my income has grown more than 600%, an astounding increase, and one that I believe can be linked to the insights I've gained through The Winning Mind Set. The information you teach in it is invaluable, and deserves to be heard by the broadest audience possible."
William Faucette, Jr.
Founder of the Millionaires Club

"The Winning Mind Set was one of the best time investments I have made in my life. Thanks!"
Barbara Zangerl, Ph.D.

"Mindset and mental preparation play a huge role in gymnastics. On a personal note, I had a PERSONAL BEST PERFORMANCE on vault this year, broke the Cornell school record, WON the Ivy League Championships, and received ALL-AMERICAN HONORS at the USAG Collegiate Nationals! I was pleasantly surprised that the techniques WORKED!"
Rachel Goldberg
Cornell Gymnastics Team Member
2004 All American Gymnast

"The Winning Mind Set has offered some excellent concepts on self-development that can be applied to any aspect of your life. I have found a number of great ideas that I believe are going to increase my successes in all aspects of my life. Fantastic!"
Bert Adams
Fitness Trainer, Cornell Fitness Centers

The "Winning Mind Set" has astounded me from the very first chapter. It's realistic approach to helping you find your true driving force is amazingly simple, yet profoundly productive! The "Winning Mind Set" challenges you to reach to the very core of your desires.
Mari Kudla
IFBB Pro Figure

"I'm out here training at the Canadian National Cycling center and next year I should be racing with the National team. It's been pretty amazing how much things have changed over the last two years. In 2003, I was struggling just to finish in local races at the lowest category. This summer I was racing against the best in North America. I truly believe that this turnaround was due in large part to the mental skills that you taught. My training may not have changed very much, but my attitude towards my training and racing was entirely different. I consider the skills that you helped teach me to be some of my most valuable assets as an athlete."

Trevor Connor
Canadian National Cycling Team

"The Winning Mind Set is one of the most significant learning experiences I have had in my life. Within any sport, most athletes and coaches will agree that our performance is dependent on our mental state at least as much as our physical state. Despite this commonly accepted fact, we typically do not spend enough time training our minds. The "Winning Mind Set" fills this gap. I went into the course expecting to learn some quick techniques, but instead I received a much more valuable lesson—it changed my whole paradigm for what is and what isn't possible."

Michael Donikian
Team Captain, Sport Taekwondo at Cornell (2002-2003)

"The 'Winning Mind Set' has been a tremendous asset to our program! We have implemented many of the concepts in the program and have used them to develop strategies to motivate and inspire our athletic teams to strive for excellence in every area of their lives. In our philosophy, the "intangible" aspects of training and team-building are just as important as the tangible. I would recommend this program to anyone interested in realizing their potential in competitive situations."

Thomas K. Howley
Assistant Athletic Director for Athlete Performance
Head Strength and Conditioning Coach
Cornell University

Also by Jim Brault

Lessons from the Masters: Seven Keys to Peak Performance and Inner Peace

Also by Kevin Seaman

Jun Fan Gung Fu Seeking The Path of Jeet Kune Do

Published by Center Line Press
PO Box762
Cortland, NY 13045

Printed in the United States of America.
Library of Congress Catalog Number: 2007900163
ISBN: 978-0-9663482-1-7
Center Line Press
PO Box762
Cortland, NY 13045

Cover Photo : ©istockphoto.com / Paulus Rusyanto, Australia
Cover Design: Scott Crist, Kevin Seaman and Karl Gesslein
Back Cover Photo of Jim Brault: Scott Crist
Back Cover Photo of Kevin Seaman: Industrial Color Labs
Visit us at www.thewinningmindset.com

Contents

*This book is dedicated to the countless amazing individuals
who have inspired us with their Winning Mind Set*

ACKNOWLEDGEMENTS

Jim Brault

To my wife Jessie and our children, Rachel, Dave and Danny – you mean the world to me.

To my father, and the spirit of my mother, thank you for your positive outlook on life, your guidance, your strong values, and your love.

To Sifu Francis Fong, I can't thank you enough for all that you have done for me. Your wisdom, energy, enthusiasm and focus serve as a daily inspiration.

To Jeff McLeod, your love of people and sheer joy in uplifting others serves as shining example to so many. I feel honored and blessed to have you as a friend.

To Kevin Seaman, thank you for your unfailing energy and dedication to improving the lives of others. I am fortunate to have you as my teacher and friend.

Finally, and most importantly, thanks to God for His many blessings.

Kevin Seaman

I once heard that life is a journey, not a destination. My incredible journey on the road to the personal development of my life has been very unique, enlightening and rewarding. There have been so many people who have influenced and inspired me. Some were teachers, some were students and many were friends and colleagues. Thank you to you all.

Most influential were my parents. Thank you for your patience and guidance. Thank you for providing a loving home and teaching me through your actions. Second is my teacher and mentor, Dan Inosanto. Your knowledge and wisdom is beyond description. Thank you for everything you've given me; you are truly an amazing man. To Francis Fong and Ajarn Chai Sirisute, you have both helped me to become who I am, thank you.

To my son, Erik, I've seen the results of your Winning Mind Set, I'm very proud of your accomplishments and who you've become. To Donna, thank you for your love and support.

Thanks to Donna Fritz for help with editing and Karl Gesslein for assistance on the cover design.

Last to my partner, Jim Brault, both my teacher and my student, thank you for your dedication to helping others, your insight, creativity and most of all, your friendship.

Chapter One

What lies within

*If we all did the things we are capable of doing,
we would literally astound ourselves.*

-THOMAS A. EDISON

A few years back, Ed the lumberjack goes into the local trading post to stock up on supplies. Bill, the owner says, to him, "You've got to try this new invention called the chainsaw. I'll guarantee it will cut 40 trees a day." Since Ed was cutting only 20 trees a day, 40 sounded like a pretty good deal to him, so he took the chain saw.

The next week Ed brings it in and asks for his money back. "I tried my best, Bill, but the most I could cut was 20, no better than my regular saw."

Bill looks at the saw, sees that the teeth are sharp, and scratches his head. "Ed, would you try it for just one more week? Give it your best shot. If it doesn't cut 40 trees a day, I'll give you your money back just like I said."

Ed gives it another week, and he puts everything he has into it. But despite his best effort he still only gets to 25 a day. He puts it on the counter and tells Bill about his results.

Bill looks it over and says, "I can't imagine why you only got 25. The other lumberjacks I've sold this to have all told me they are cutting at least 40 trees a day." He primes the engine, and pulls the cord, and the chainsaw starts right up.

Ed says; puzzled, "What's that noise?"

You possess incredible potential. As a human being you have been endowed with a capacity that is nothing short of astounding: a capacity to learn, to grow, to develop, to think, to create, to change, to love, to act and to impact that is truly amazing. But like Ed, many of us fail to maximize our potential. Sometimes it's because we don't know to pull the cord; in other words, we don't know what our potential even is. Other times we know what it is, and have even have demonstrated that potential, but we don't do it consistently for a whole variety of reasons. It's as if we have a gas powered saw that we use without turning on.

In the joke we began with, the failure to capitalize on the potential of the chainsaw is amusing; in individuals, that failure to maximize potential can mean poverty, stress, unhappiness, loneliness, despair, regret and a lack of fulfillment. In organizations, that failure to capitalize on potential can manifest as lower revenues, reduced margins, higher turnover, and customer and employee dissatisfaction. In society at large these effects are magnified and result in an unbelievable waste of the most valuable resource we have, the vast expanse of human potential. In the theme of the United Negro College Fund slogan, "Potential" is a terrible thing to waste.

This book is all about sharing with you proven tools and techniques to help you to "turn on the power", the transformative power of your mind so that you can enjoy and share the benefits of your unique gifts and talents however those manifest, whether that is to better help the company you work for, achieve a level of financial success you desire, or to start a foundation that benefits underprivileged youth. Maybe you want to achieve your athletic goals; to get in the best shape of your life, or be the kind of boss, spouse, parent or friend that you aspire to be. You probably yearn for a good balance in your life, and want to "succeed" in many areas of your life.

Whether your goals are long term or more how you want to be "in the moment", we believe that the ***Winning Mind Set***^{TM} tools and techniques can help you because we have witnessed first hand the positive results of applying these tools with literally thousands of people we have had the privilege of working with over the years.

Where did these tools come from?

The question of human potential and the variability of behavior, (i.e., why we do and don't do certain things at any given moment) has been a passion of ours for over 25 years. Initially, we were focused more on our own lives. As athletes, there were times when we performed at our best, and times when we didn't do as well as we could have given our abilities at that given point in time, so we were very interested in how to perform at our best when we needed to. Similarly, in our personal lives we wanted to be a certain way with those closest to us; professionally, we strove to succeed financially in various businesses endeavors. Some of our aspirations for success were measured by the hard metrics of revenue, margin, customer retention and customer loyalty. In athletics, success was measured by wins, and in the relationships with our families success was gauged by the softer yet even more important qualities of patience, support and love.

I have had more trouble with myself
Than with any person I have ever met.

-DWIGHT MOODY

As a result, we began to study human behavior from a variety of perspectives, including what was at that time called psychosomatic medicine. Of particular interest was the role of the mind in the healing process, the placebo effect, and the relationship of the patient to the physician. As Dr. Norman Cousins and others began to reveal that a positive outlook could affect something as objectively real and potentially devastating as cancer, an entire new field of study developed. Now known as psychoneuroimmunology, this field investigates the relationship between physical health and beliefs, expectations, associations, emotions and learning, and has helped to shift the approaches that many professionals in the field are now taking toward health care. It has also helped to transform the role of the patient from that of a submissive respondent to an active participant.

Drugs are not always necessary,
(but) belief in recovery always is.

-NORMAN COUSINS

In researching the applications of these ideas at collegiate, Olympic and professional levels in sports, we found that coaches and trainers had teamed up with scientists to determine how mental imagery and conditioned responses affect brain wave patterns, which in turn affect the body and its functioning. Neuroscientists have shown that mental practice can actually increase objective physical strength and performance. Mental imagery or visualization activates many of the same neural circuits in the visual cortex that actual sight does. Imagining and rehearsing what it feels like to perform certain movements stimulates the same circuits in the motor cortex of the brain that actual movement does. It is for these reasons that the U.S. Olympic Committee went from one full-time sports psychologist in 1988 to five in 2000.

We immersed ourselves in the study of such topics as exercise physiology, developmental, behavioral, physiological and clinical psychology, training and development, organizational behavior and organization development, team dynamics, and leadership coaching, as well as Neuro-Linguistic Programming (NLP), Neuro-Associative Conditioning ™, meditation, hypnotherapy, yoga, qigong, internal and external martial arts, and psychophysical re-education all in an effort to learn how the mind effects performance and behavior.

Just as we had initially wanted to help improve our own lives, we became increasingly interested in helping others to tap into and more effectively direct and control the power of their minds to have a winning mindset, whether that be on the field, in the classroom, at home, or on the job.

Over the years, with students, athletes, our own children, salespeople, employees, managers and executives, we have tested the concepts and approaches from these varied fields with literally thousands of people, in one-on-one sessions, group-training programs, in the corporate world and at Cornell University. Frankly, at first, a good portion of this application was trial and error, of seeing which methods worked best with different people in varying environments and situations. Over time, though, we have honed and modified these techniques and approaches to single out the ones that have proven to yield the best results in helping people see positive results in their lives. With such tools and techniques, our "students" have obtained incredible and rewarding results, including:

- Being able to better deal with daily stress and changes
- Breaking through barriers and limits
- Learning more quickly and effectively
- Taking action in areas that have been difficult in the past
- Overcoming procrastination
- Improving ability and ease in public speaking and presentations
- Increasing sales by an average of 47%
- Making significant life and career changes
- Achieving business and personal goals
- Increasing levels of self-motivation
- Gaining confidence
- Being able to relax more quickly and completely
- Losing weight
- Quitting smoking and other habits
- Gaining a better work /life balance

What you now hold in your hands, then, is a compilation of these approaches. It is a set of tools designed to be both easy to understand and easy to put into action. In fact, to make it simple for you to remember, we have codified the *Winning Mind Set™ techniques* into the acronym **BEHAVIOR™**:

*B*eliefs

*E*motions

*H*abits

*A*ssociations

*V*alues

*I*dentity

*O*bjectives

*R*einforcement

While these approaches are grouped in a certain way, starting at Belief and ending in Reinforcement, the order is for the purpose of remembering the categories. You don't necessarily have to go straight through as it is written, but at least in your first read it probably makes the most sense to do so. Here's why.

A lot of people want to start out with **Objectives** - after all goal setting is very powerful and can serve to harness and focus your mind. But haven't you set goals in the past and then not followed through? We have. Many times it is because the goals we set are not aligned with our core **Values**, those attributes that are most important to us in our lives. Understanding what drives you at your core (your value system) is foundational to establishing powerful and motivating goals. Otherwise, you'll set a bunch of goals that you don't end up doing, or you do achieve them and say, "Is that it?" Therefore, being clear about your value system is crucial.

On the other hand, you may have a goal that is aligned with your value system, but you don't totally believe it is possible for you to attain. What you'll probably end up doing is giving it a half hearted attempt because deep down you don't truly believe that your efforts will bear fruit so at some point, consciously or subconsciously, you'll say, "Why bother?"

You could also set great goals that are aligned with your beliefs, but you let your **Emotions** get the best of you, and then in that state (angry, sad, frustrated, dejected, overwhelmed, etc.) not be motivated to follow through on the actions it will take to get achieve your goal. Your emotional state could be altered through the questions you ask yourself, the pattern of language you use, the way you use your body in empowering or de-energizing ways, or through negative anchors (a learned response through **Association**).

It is also beneficial to understand which **Habits** are useful and productive in helping you reach success as you define it, and also learn how to extinguish negative habits that may be holding you back. You will also benefit from ensuring that your **Identity** aligns with your value system and goals, otherwise it can be like you are living two lives. Finally, it is critical that you ensure that you **Reinforce** new behaviors, through positive associations, visual aids, and / or a support structure.

Suffice it to say that these tools and techniques are intertwined and can't be separated in actual practice. Just as physically the cardiac, pulmonary, endocrine, nervous, muscular, skeletal, and digestive systems are all related, human behavior is complex and is impossible to reduce to a single driving force.

Our suggestion to you is to go through the book as it is laid out, assimilating the concepts and working through the exercises in each section, and then go back and revisit certain portions again as desired. In so doing, you will establish what is most important to you in your life, will understand the skills and competencies needed to achieve your goals, and will possess an arsenal of tools to help motivate and support you in being the kind of person you want to be and accomplishing the things you want to do - a success.

Before you begin to learn about the **Winning Mind Set**^{TM}, we would like to express our admiration for you. Regardless of how great your life might be right now, you are committed to continuous improvement and to maximizing the potential that you were given. In that way we are kindred spirits, and we hope that you will find tremendous value in the ideas expressed in the pages that follow.

Let's get started!

What lies behind us, and what lies before us,
Are tiny matters compared to what lies within us.

-OLIVER WENDELL HOLMES

Chapter Two

Beliefs

They conquer who believe they can.

-RALPH WALDO EMERSON

Beliefs are one of the most powerful forces that exist to motivate an individual, a team, or a nation.

A belief that love would overcome hate, and that non-violent opposition would overcome British rule is what motivated Gandhi and his followers to endure beatings without fighting back.

A belief that it was possible to invent the incandescent light bulb is what allowed Thomas Alva Edison to persevere after 10,000 "failed" attempts.

A belief is what allowed Neil Armstrong to take that "giant step for mankind."

And a belief is what allowed a man named Roger Bannister to make history. Roger Bannister was a world-class runner, and the first person to break the four-minute mile barrier. Up until that time, no person on earth had ever run a mile in under four minutes. In fact, physicians and trainers declared that it was physiologically impossible for a human being to run that fast. Yet, Roger knew that he could do it, and in fact in 1954 achieved his goal. He did it using two approaches.

First, he put in his running shoe a slip of paper with "3:58" written on it. Every time he ran, he had that little piece of paper as a reminder of his goal, utilizing the **power of visualization**. Second, he broke this seemingly impenetrable obstacle into smaller chunks. Specifically, instead of thinking about the goal in terms of minutes, he broke it down into 240 seconds. As he ran and got closer to the goal, he thought that he could shave it off by just a fraction of a second. After all, less than one second wasn't that big a deal. So instead of going directly from where he was to where he wanted to be in his mind, he took it in little steps, a fraction of a second at a time.

What Roger Bannister did was certainly impressive. What happened *after* he broke the record is even more so. Remember that until he broke the four-minute mile barrier, no one else had ever done it. But within one year, 37 other runners did the same thing. In the year after that, over 300 runners ran a mile in less than four minutes.

Every one of those runners had within themselves the capability to achieve that goal. Each one of them had the potential to run that fast, but it wasn't until someone else showed them that it was possible, it wasn't until they believed it, that they tapped into the potential that was always there.

It isn't until we believe that we begin to tap into our true potential.

How can you tap into and direct the power of beliefs in your life? To answer that question, let's explore beliefs in more detail and start with a definition. According to Webster's Dictionary, a belief is "a state of habit of mind in which trust or confidence is placed in some person or thing." It is a *feeling* of confidence or certainty in truth. A belief, in fact, is not necessarily true or factual. But, the person having such a belief act as if it is indeed true.

"Believe it! High expectations are the KEY to everything.

-SAM WALTON

Categories

There are two major types of beliefs. We call the first kind *If / Then Beliefs*, literally because of the way they are structured in the English language:

1. *If* I work hard, *then* I'll get ahead.
2. *If* I'm good, Santa Claus will bring me presents (sometimes the "then" is implied).
3. *If* I work out every day, *then* I'll be healthier.
4. *If* I treat others the way I want to be treated, *then* they will treat me the same way (the Golden Rule).
5. *If* she can do it, *then* I know I can, too.
6. It doesn't matter if I drop out of school since I'm not going anywhere anyway. (Many statements have the "if / then" structure reformatted – *If* I drop out of school *then* it won't matter since I don't have a future anyway).

The other major type of beliefs we call *Categorical Beliefs*. These are broad generalizations about an entire category:

1. Big companies are ...
2. Life is ...

3. Americans are ...

4. Religions are ...

5. Chinese food is ...

6. Politicians are ...

7. Younger people are ...

8. Older people are ...

9. Vegetarians are ...

10. Engineers are ...

In some respects these are stereotypes, especially about people.

Structure and References

A belief is a feeling of confidence or certainty with *If / Then* and *Categorical Beliefs*. To better understand how our beliefs are established we'll use the simple analogy we learned from Tony Robbins.

What makes the top of a table just that as opposed to a piece of wood, metal or glass lying on the floor? Legs, of course. The "legs" that support a belief are called references. These references literally support that feeling of certainty. The analogy, then, is that references are to a belief as legs are to a table. Without legs you have a tabletop lying on the floor; without references for support, you basically have an opinion or an idea, not a belief, not a feeling of certainty.

There are three kinds of references.

1. **Personal References** are those gained from experiences that actually happened to you personally.

2. **Second-hand References** are gained through others, what people tell you (parents, teachers, friends, religious authorities, relatives, neighbors, co-workers), what you read (magazines, newspapers, religious materials,

textbooks, e-mail, internet, novels, etc.), what you see (television, movies, plays), and so forth.

3. **Imagined References** are just that, imagined. You don't actually experience an event or feeling, but you imagine it in your subconscious (it could be from a dream, or simply created in your mind).

"When you believe in something, and you carry it in your heart, you accept no excuses, only results."

-KEN BLANCHARD

Let's put all of these concepts together by looking at a common example. Did you believe in Santa Claus as a child? Were you convinced that he would come down your chimney on Christmas Eve and put presents under the tree, fill up your stocking, and eat the cookies and drink the milk that you left him? You probably did.

Why did you believe in him? Well, for one thing you got presents from Santa Claus, right? That would be a personal reference because you personally received gifts. One table leg.
You also went to visit Santa at a store or a mall, and you gave him a list of things you wanted. Also a personal reference, and another table leg.

Your parents told you there was a Santa Claus, and that you had to be a good little girl or boy to get what you wanted (an If / Then belief: if you were good, then you would get presents), with a second-hand reference coming from your parents. Two more table legs.

You also heard stories about Santa, may have sang songs about Santa, watched movies about Santa, wrote letters to Santa at school, saw that Santa ate your cookies and maybe wrote a note thanking you. Second-hand references, and so many legs you lost count.

Finally, your imagination ran wild. Every year you swore you heard reindeer on your roof, and you thought you heard Santa downstairs. Powerful imagined references, even though your table hardly needs any more legs. Getting the picture?

So, why do you no longer believe in Santa Claus? What happened to change such a strong belief? Did the change happen in one fell swoop? Probably not. A more likely scenario was that one by one, your references were wiped out. Maybe kids at school started telling you that there was no such thing as Santa Claus. One leg gone, but still many left. Then perhaps your brother, sister, cousin or friend told you he didn't exist, and another leg went. Then maybe you noticed that the wrapping paper that Santa used was the same as what your parents used, and the Santa at the mall didn't look so real, and pretty soon you didn't have too many more legs, and the ones you did have were pretty wobbly. Without references, your feeling of certainty was gone, and so was the belief.

Make sense? As a concept, it's pretty easy: a structure of legs and a tabletop, references and beliefs. Now, what are the effects of beliefs?

Effects of Empowering and Limiting Beliefs

Experience is not what happens to a man.
It is what a man does with what happens to him.

-ALDOUS HUXLEY

Beliefs can either **empower** us to tap into our potential and go beyond what others may have ever thought possible, or limit us tremendously, holding us back from achieving things that are well within our potential because of self-defeating doubts and fears.

Examples of articulated Empowering Beliefs are:

1. If I did it before, I can do it again.
2. I know it's possible.
3. There has to be a way.
4. If I have succeeded in other things, I'm sure I can do it now, too.
5. I have all the tools I need; it will just take time, perseverance and patience.

Empowering beliefs:

- Allow us to tap into our vast potential.
- Help us to ask better questions to access resources that can help us reach our goal. (Who can help? What do we need to do first? Who has already done this, or something like this, that we can contact? What are we overlooking?)
- Encourage us to look for a solution instead of quitting when we face challenges.

Credendo Vides! By believing one sees.
It's tattooed on my ankle for a reason.
Success is never something found alone.

— EMERY MILLER, IFBB PROFESSIONAL

Tapping into Our Vast Potential

What did Roger Bannister's beliefs allow him to do? They allowed him to achieve a feat that no one on earth ever had before. He had an If /Then Belief (you can imagine his internal dialogue being something like, "If I can run a mile in 244 seconds, then I'm sure I can do it in 243, and if I can run it in 243, I'm sure I can knock off one more second, after all it's only one more second, how hard can that be?") that helped him to focus on tiny, continuous improvement. He also utilized imagined references to harness the power of visualization. Since no one else had ever run a mile in less than four minutes before, he had to imagine it was possible, he had to create such a level of certainty in his entire being, his entire nervous system and subconscious that he knew, he absolutely *knew*, that running a mile in less than four minutes was not only possible, but that he *personally* could do it.

By the way, can your subconscious mind, the part of you that really runs things (and this is not just your brain, but your entire interconnected system, much of which is below your conscious awareness), can it distinguish between something that actually happened to you and something you imagined? Before you answer, have you ever had a dream where you wake up and feel as if what you just dreamt about had actually occurred? Where your heart is beating out of your chest, you may be sweating, anxious, excited, or petrified? No doubt, and could your subconscious tell the difference? No way. Our subconscious does not distinguish between something we vividly imagine, and something that we actually experience.

Roger Bannister's beliefs enabled him to tap a potential in his body that was always there; these beliefs inspired and empowered him to achieve a feat greater than he or anyone else had ever before accomplished.

> *"The biggest thing is to have a mind-set and*
> *a belief you can win every tournament going in."*
>
> - TIGER WOODS

Accessing Resources

Have you ever had the experience where you get a new car, and then wherever you go, your car seems to be everywhere? Or if someone close to you is pregnant (or yourself), then you seem to see pregnant women everywhere? This heightened awareness is a result of the workings of a part of the brain near the brainstem called the Reticular Activating System, or RAS.

The RAS has the job of sorting out literally millions of bits of information for the brain to focus on and process. We would go crazy if it weren't for the RAS; our conscious mind would be overwhelmed. The RAS limits what we consciously focus on, kind of like a bouncer at the door of a nightclub who only lets in a few select people. This sorting out process allows us to focus our senses on things that we believe have value to us (our new car, pregnancy), that we feel are important (women have a keener sense for higher pitched sounds, like babies' crying, while men have more sensitivity to lower pitched sounds, the sound of other males who could be potential threats), as well as stimuli that are consistent with our beliefs. It's not that these stimuli weren't there before; it's just that our RAS didn't allow them all to surface to the level of our conscious awareness.

Our beliefs determine what we do and do not see.

If you have a belief that something is possible, you are sending a signal to your RAS to be on the lookout for anything or anyone that can help you in your quest. Again, it is similar to giving a bouncer a list of people who can come in. Your list would say, "Anyone who can help me with this issue can come in." If you didn't have that belief, then even if people were in the crowd waiting to help, you would not allow them access.

Look for Solutions

If you believe something is possible, your mind will work overtime to come up with solutions by asking better questions. If you don't believe it is possible, then you are sending a signal to your mind that says, "This is not achievable, focus on something else." If you aren't sure whether or not something is possible, then your mind is divided, partly accepting, partly negating your belief (you'll find out more about how powerful the effects of a divided mind are when we get to Emotions). If, on the other hand, you feel totally confident in your belief, then you send a signal to your brain that sends the message, "This is possible. Figure out any and all ways to make this come true."

Out of that belief, you can come up with better questions like:

- Who can help me / us?
- Who has done this before?

- What approaches seem to work best? Which ones don't seem to work as well?
- What should I / we do first? What should I do right now?

What about Limiting Beliefs? What do they hold us back from doing? What do you think having a limiting belief does to your nervous system? Think about it. How come 37 runners somehow mysteriously broke the 4-minute mile after Roger Bannister did it within a year? Did they suddenly get stronger? Well, actually, yes. But it had absolutely nothing to do with their body, and had everything to do with their expanded beliefs, which allowed their minds and bodies to achieve something that they heretofore thought impossible.

Did every one of the 37 runners who broke the four-minute mile in the year after Roger Bannister did have the potential to do it? Of course they did. But until he did it, until they had that second-hand reference that allowed them to believe it was possible, they didn't utilize their full potential.

Most people are not aware of the degree to which limiting beliefs hold us back. Consider phrases like these:
- There's no way we can do it.
- I could never do that.
- I don't think it's possible.
- We can never recapture what we had.
- I've never been able to before, why should this time be any different?
- They don't let people like me do that.
- Our organization will never change.
- The boss will never go for that.
- I'm not _____ enough (smart, strong, old, wealthy, fast, etc.)

- I'm too _____ (young, old, slow, poor, etc.)
- Maybe someone else can do that, but not me. I don't have the background.

What is each of these saying? Forget saying, *screaming?* I / WE DON"T BELIEVE IT IS POSSIBLE! or IT MAY BE POSSIBLE, BUT I / WE CAN'T DO IT!

Limiting beliefs:

- Cause us to ignore opportunities by not focusing our minds on solutions
- Create a sense of false limits about our abilities, talents and power
- Limit our potential

Ignoring opportunities

You'll see it when you believe it.

-WAYNE DYER

Without positive beliefs, you will miss opportunities. What does that mean? Have you ever had an experience like this? Your mom asks you to get the ketchup. You reply, "We don't have any ketchup. I used up the last bottle," to which she says that there indeed is ketchup and please go get it. So you humph over to wherever it is "supposed" to be, give a perfunctory look around, and proudly proclaim in your best I- told- you- so voice, "There isn't any."

With perhaps some firm and rapid steps she comes right up behind you, reaches forward, and grabs a bottle of ketchup that just "magically" appeared before your very eyes and says, "What is *this*?" "Oh, ketchup ... I thought you said ..."

It's happened to all of us. In fact, you may be happy to know that it happens so often that there is even a psychological term for it. It's called a **scotoma**, a term used for a blind spot in an otherwise normal vision field.

In this case a scotoma is when your brain does not allow you to perceive something that you do not believe exists. What you believe determines what you perceive, again linked to the RAS we talked about before.

If you don't believe something exists, then how much effort are you going to put into looking for it? Little, if any. If you don't think something is possible, how much time are you going to spend trying to figure it out? Again, not too much. If you don't think you are capable of doing something, are you even going to bother? Or is it more likely that you will figure, "Why waste my time?"

> *Our doubts are traitors,*
> *and make us lose the good we oft might win,*
> *by fearing to attempt.*
>
> -WILLIAM SHAKESPEARE

False Limits and Learned Helplessness

The danger with limiting beliefs is that we can fall into a trap of holding ourselves back very quickly. Consider these examples of a phenomenon known as "learned helplessness":

When circus elephants are very young, the handlers put an iron manacle and chain around one of their legs. The chain is attached to a stake, which is pounded into the ground. The young elephant will pull and pull against the stake, and in fact rub the skin raw trying to get away. But after a period of time it learns that it is not strong enough to break free and stops trying.

A full-grown elephant is more than strong enough to pull out the stake, but doesn't. Why not? Because the elephant has learned through personal references or experience that it cannot break free, it doesn't even try.

Research has been done with fish in aquariums where a glass barrier is inserted into the tank. After a period of time, the fish learn that there is a point that they cannot go beyond. Once they learn that, even after it is removed, they still do not go beyond that point. This now imagined barrier prevents them from venturing forth.

If you have an electric fence for your dog, you have probably experienced the same type of learned response. Your dog will learn where it cannot go, and will not go beyond that point because it believes it will experience the pain of an electric shock. A lot of times dog owners will say that the collar hasn't had batteries in it for years, but the belief that crossing that line will lead to pain still holds the dog back.

Another research study offers a prime example of this phenomenon of learned helplessness. Researchers took a number of dogs, and randomly divided them into three groups. Each group was placed on one side of a room. In the middle of the room was a small barrier, one that the dogs could easily jump over.

Group A was put into the room and left for a period of time. After a while the dogs jumped back and forth over the barrier, until the researchers took them out and replaced them with Group B. This group, however, was treated differently. The floor of the first side of the room for this group was electrified, and the dogs received a mild electric shock. Wanting to avoid the pain, the dogs in Group B jumped over the barrier. When they got to the other side, there was no shock. When the researchers put them back on the first side, they immediately jumped over to avoid the pain of the shock.

Group C was not as lucky. For this group, both sides were electrified. These dogs, too, jumped over the barrier, but when they got to the other side, they still received the shocks. Regardless of where they went, they got the pain of the shock.

The next day, the researchers took the same three groups of dogs and put each group into a *different* room than they had been in on the previous day, one with a *smaller* barrier. But this time, all three groups had the same conditions: the first side was electrified, and the second side wasn't.

So what do you think Group A did? Remember, they had never received the shocks before. When the dogs did get shocked, they jumped over the barrier in an attempt to get away from the pain. Group B did exactly the same thing as they had the day before. Their belief was that the first side equals pain, the second side doesn't.

What do you think Group C did? Nothing. They sat there. Why? Because they believed, they felt certain that it didn't matter what they did, since regardless of where they went, they would encounter pain, so why bother? Even though this was a different room, a different barrier, and a different situation, their limiting belief caused them not to take action to prevent a situation that they were absolutely capable of avoiding.

In each of these examples, the animals had personal references about their given situations. They actually experienced a genuine limitation. But the problem comes along when instead of these limits being confined to just these experiences in a specific situation, or a single time, or at a certain location, they extrapolated these references to cover all similar experiences. Thus, they learned to be helpless in situations where they were truly not.

Now, it would be easy to say that these examples are with animals, and that we humans are much smarter, wouldn't it? It would be easy to say that people are much more intelligent than this, and that we would never allow ourselves to be limited by such references. But if we are honest, we know that just isn't true.

How many times have we held ourselves back from trying things we could absolutely do, just because our inner voice said that we couldn't? How many times have we thought "This will never work", or "I've already tried this", and given up, or worse, never even attempted because of something in our past that made us believe that we couldn't do it?

Limiting Our Potential

Empowering beliefs have an incredible power to lift us to new heights, while limiting beliefs have the ability to hold us down and prevent us from being what we could be.

Some people would say that limiting beliefs protect us from pain, real and imagined. For example, one might point out that people on heroin often are in a state of euphoria and believe that they can fly. They leap off buildings and, of course, plummet to their deaths. These types of beliefs are really more disturbances, pathological psychology, and not the subject we are talking about here. But while we're at it, if the Wright brothers never believed that humans could fly, would they ever have invented the airplane?

How Beliefs Affect Actions

Now that we've spent a little bit of time laying a foundation for understanding beliefs, it's time to start working through some exercises.

List out the empowering beliefs that you feel have really made you who you are, and which have allowed you to take action in areas where others may have held themselves back. If you have trouble coming up with what they are, think about things that you do, activities you pursue, and goals you have attained, that sort of thing. Consider your beliefs about time, money, energy, age, experience, knowledge, and people. Here are a few examples to get you started:

Empowering Beliefs

1. Exercising is fun.
2. I can do anything I put my mind to.
3. People are generally nice if you give them a chance.
4. I am a good parent.
5. I know I can win.
6. I can do more the next time.
7. I have the time and energy for anything I really care about.
8. I can get the money for whatever I really am committed to.
9. If I persevere, I can learn anything.

Winning Mind Set™ Exercise

Assessing Our Empowering Beliefs and Supporting References

List out the top five or six empowering beliefs that have made the most significant difference in your life so far:

Now, as you look at your list, determine what types of references you have to support your beliefs. Notice if your references have any pattern to them. That is, do they tend to be personal, second-hand, or imagined references? There is no right or wrong, simply notice them. Again, here is an example to give you the idea.

"Exercising is fun. I believe this because I have years of personal references. I enjoy how I feel during exercise and afterwards, and I get to meet a lot of great people in the process. People I work out with also seem to have fun, too, and that is a second-hand reference, but for me my primary references are personal."

Okay? So go ahead and list them out:

Supporting References

It's easy to for us to focus on the references that support our beliefs. But let's take a closer look by using the example of exercising:

> "*Exercising is fun.* I believe this because I have years of personal references. I enjoy how I feel during exercise and afterwards, and I get to meet a lot of great people in the process. People I work out with also seem to have fun, and that is a second-hand reference, but for me my primary references are personal."

Were there ever times when exercising wasn't fun for this person? (Let's assume it was written by a woman). Of course there were. Were there times when she got injured? Was that fun, too? Probably not. Did she ever feel nauseous during or after exercise? What about sore? Was that a good time? Did she ever meet people that were not great?

We tend to remember or focus on those references that are consistent with our beliefs. That is, even if we use personal references to support our belief, we don't use all of our personal references. Instead, we focus on only a portion of them, or we tend to minimize the negatives (as in the above example, injury, nausea, difficulty), and accentuate the positives. Remember the ketchup and scotoma?

Our use of references is selective, and tends to be skewed. Bear this in mind when you work through your limiting beliefs. But let's get back to your list of empowering beliefs right now. For each of your empowering beliefs, ask yourself what are the benefits of having a belief like that? What does it allow you to do? What do you think you would never had tried or accomplished if not for having this feeling of certainty? Again, an example:

"I can do anything I put my mind to. I believe this based on personal references. I have succeeded in athletics and business, even in those instances where I had absolutely no background from which to work. The benefits of having this belief is that I am not hesitant to try new things and am confident that I can figure them out. If I need help, I will ask, since I am confident that I can succeed. I also know that if I break a new endeavor down into little steps, am patient, and keep persisting, that I will succeed. So, I adapt to change readily, and feel comfortable in new situations.

"I also have many second-hand references of friends and acquaintances that have succeeded in endeavors once they put their minds to their task.

"If I didn't have this belief, I probably would never have started my own business."

You try it.

Benefits I've Obtained From My Empowering Beliefs

Limiting Beliefs

Now, list out those limiting beliefs that you feel have held you back, those that have prevented you from taking action in areas that are or were important to you. If you have trouble coming up with what they are, think about things that you want but don't have (material things, feelings, accomplishments), or things that you *say* you want to do that you don't (activities you don't pursue or "find the time for"). Think about what your beliefs are around time, money, energy, age, experience, knowledge, relationships, and people. Here again are a few examples of the some common limiting beliefs:

Limiting beliefs

- Exercising is painful, and I'm too out of shape to begin.
- I don't have enough experience to teach.
- You can't trust people.
- I'm terrible in relationships.
- I don't think I can beat …
- I don't have enough time.
- I'll never get back to where I was.
- I don't think I can do it again.
- I'm in a rut.
- S/he is too strong / fast / skilled (or, I'm not strong / fast / skilled enough to win)
- I don't have enough money.
- I'm too (old, young, short, tall, fat, skinny …)
- I don't have the energy to learn anything new.

Winning Mind Set™ Exercise

Assessing Our Empowering Beliefs and Supporting References

List out the top five or six beliefs that you think have limited you the most:

As you look at your list, determine what types of references you have to support these beliefs. As you list them out, notice if the references for your limiting beliefs have a pattern to them, personal, second-hand, or imagined references. Are the references the same type or different from those that support your empowering beliefs?

An example:

> **"Exercising is painful, and I'm too out of shape to begin.** I believe this based on personal and second-hand references. I tried working out a number of times. Once I tried running, and ended up with shin splints. Another time I lifted weights, and I was so sore afterwards that I couldn't walk normally for almost a week. A few friends of mine tried working out, too, but they didn't see any results, so they stopped. I don't want to go to a gym because everyone there is in shape, and I am embarrassed by the way I look."

Personal references: got hurt running, sore after lifting weights, embarrassed by looks.

Second-hand references: friends said they tried it but didn't see any results.

Imagined references: everyone there is in shape.

For each of those five or six beliefs that limit you the most list the supporting references for them:

Supporting References

With any beliefs, it's easy to focus on the references that support them. Just as we did with the empowering beliefs about exercising, let's take a closer look at the example of limiting beliefs about exercising:

> **"Exercising is painful, and I'm too out of shape to begin.** I believe this based on personal and second-hand references. I tried working out a number of times. Once I tried running, and ended up with shin splints. Another time I lifted weights, and I was so sore afterwards that I couldn't walk normally for almost a week. A few friends of mine tried working out, too, but they didn't see any results, so they stopped. I don't want to go to a gym because everyone there is in shape, and I am embarrassed by how I look."

Was there ever any time that this person enjoyed exercising? Maybe her idea of exercising is too narrow. What about swimming, or walking? Has she ever done that and enjoyed it? Does she have a dog that she walks? Was it possible that she didn't have the proper shoes to run in, or that she was lifting weights improperly, or started off too quickly?

Did she ever talk with someone who enjoyed exercising? Did she ever read about people who do? Bought a book or exercise tape? Hired a personal trainer? Is it possible that there are gyms or other places to work out where the clients are more "like her"? What about exercises like yoga or T'ai Chi? Is it possible that she would feel more comfortable in these type of classes and not be embarrassed?

Do you see how you can challenge the references (remove or at least weaken the legs) in order to help change a belief? We'll get back to that.

For each of your limiting beliefs, ask yourself what the consequences are of having a belief like that. What does it hold you back from doing? What have you never tried because of this belief? Again, here is an example of how it may relate consequentially:

"I don't have enough time. This is based on personal references. My schedule is jam-packed. I am up at 5:00am every morning, and I don't get to bed until 11:00pm most nights during the week, and that's if I'm lucky. There are a whole lot of things that I would like to do. I would like to spend more time with my parents, after all they are getting older, and they may not be around much longer. I would like to spend more time with my wife and children as well, and I'm not exercising as much as I would like. This belief of not having enough time – and I certainly have the references for it – creates pressure. Whatever I'm doing I always have a sense of rushing, like there is something else I ought to be doing. At times this is frustrating to me, and I may not treat others around me the way I would like. I either am short with them, or they get a sense like I am not fully present. This constant pressure feeling of not enough time is also very tiring. When I do get a chance for a break I want to pass out!"

List out the consequences of a limiting belief that you have:

Consequences of My Limiting Beliefs

Conflicting Beliefs

Think about these "beliefs":

- Look before you leap, vs. He who hesitates is lost.
- If you want something done right, you have to do it yourself, vs. Two heads are better than one.
- Ask and you shall receive, vs. Good things come to those who wait.
- You can't teach an old dog new tricks, vs. If there is a will there is a way.

Cultural beliefs, what some might call aphorisms, often send conflicting messages as the above examples illustrate. It is quite common for us to have beliefs that conflict, especially in the important areas of relationships, money, time and energy.

For instance, you may know people who long to get into a relationship. They want to have someone to trust, to open up to and share themselves with. They desire to feel the closeness and intimacy that can be found in a relationship, yet they don't take any action towards making that desire a reality. Why not? Because they are fearful of being hurt due to the fact that they choose to focus on the bad experiences they have had in the past (personal references), and their new limiting belief may be something like "All men / women lie, or cheat, or will hurt you".

In psychology this is called "approach avoidance", where an individual experiences a pull towards something, yet at the same time feels a repulsion that pushes them away from that same thing. This is because the situation evokes multiple and conflicting emotions based on multiple and conflicting beliefs.

Another example is found with parenting. Some mothers and fathers believe that to be a good parent they have to provide for their children financially, so they work extremely hard and long hours to do that. They may hold onto beliefs such as "*If* I am a good parent, *then* I have to make enough money to send them to a good school," or may phrase it as "Good parents provide for their kids financially" (a categorical belief). Yet part of them feels guilty about being away from their kids, too (they may have an equally strong belief that "Kids are only young once, so the most important thing is to spend time with them."), and they end up with an internal battle over which approach is "right". Many two-income families struggle with this very issue.

This is a source of a lot of pain for many people, and we will get into this topic in more depth when we investigate Values, but for now, simply notice whether there are any conflicts between your empowering beliefs and your limiting beliefs. If so, take a moment and jot them down. Include any issues that this brings up for you, areas of tension, arguments, guilt, anger, or emotional drain.

Do not let what you cannot do
interfere with what you can do.

- JOHN WOODEN

Winning Mind Set™ **Exercise**
Assessing Conflicts Between Our Empowering and Limiting Beliefs

---

Possible Conflicts Between My Empowering Beliefs and My Limiting Beliefs

We've covered a lot of ground so far learning about the foundational elements of beliefs, and then discovering what some of your empowering and limiting beliefs are in order to help prepare you to assist others in this area. Up until you did this, you may not have been aware of these beliefs and the benefits or consequences of them at a conscious level.

Beliefs affect what you do or don't *do* by dictating what you will and will not even *attempt*.

As we hope you are beginning to see, making changes to your belief system can powerfully affect what you do and don't do, what you will and won't try. Certainly, as you progress in this book, you will see that all of the elements of **BEHAVIOR**™ are important, and that they intertwine. You may find that you come back to this section later on as you gain more insight into your beliefs by getting into more depth in other areas.

One last thing before we get into how to make changes in your beliefs, and that is that all beliefs are not created equal. That is, there are some beliefs that are transitory in nature. A feeling of "I can't do this!" might be a fleeting thought due to momentary jitters, overwhelm, or fatigue. Beliefs such as these may ebb and flow based on your emotions and energy levels. Given a little time, once you are in a different emotional or energetic state, your beliefs shift. So beliefs are not always these permanent feelings. They can be quite short-lived based on how we are feeling. We'll discuss ways that you can manage your energy level on a more consistent basis in the section on Emotions.

There are other beliefs, though, that are more pervasive and permanent. In this section, let's look at these since they can be more complex to deal with, and knowing how to approach them can adequately prepare you to deal with a spectrum of beliefs.

Changing Beliefs

Remember that our beliefs are based on references. Actually, what would be more accurate is to say that *our beliefs are based on the references that we choose to focus upon.* What if you have negative beliefs, or your empowering beliefs are weak? How can you make a positive and impactful change? Basically, there are four main ways to change your beliefs:

1. Reinforcing and expanding positive references
2. Challenging limiting references
3. Playing out the consequences of limiting beliefs
4. Imagining success

Reinforcing and Expanding Positive References

Positive references can be either personal or second-hand. Everybody has a whole series of personal references for success in a number of areas if they look hard enough (after all, we are all alive; that is at least *one* positive reference). An excellent way to help strengthen an existing empowering belief is to focus on personal references you already have. For example, let's say you have a certain degree of success in one arena, and are now going to a new level. You might think about or discuss with someone else what made you successful in the past:

1. When you began that endeavor, you didn't have any success yet. What did you think about or focus on that helped you succeed?
2. What did you learn in your past that you could apply here?
3. What would you have to believe for you to be successful here? (or what do you believe?)
4. Think about a time in your past when you succeeded in something that, in the beginning, you weren't sure you could pull off. How did you do that?
5. What is your proudest accomplishment? How did you go about achieving that?

By focusing on your successes in the past, this will help you reinforce references (legs) to support an already powerful belief. It will have a *carry-over* effect in that the references that supported you in the past, will also work to support you in your current endeavor (same old legs, new table top).

While personal references may be the most direct and quickest way to change a belief, you may not have a personal experience that you can transfer to a new situation, or you may have difficulty remembering an experience in a way that is empowering. You may have selective recall and, for whatever reason, focus on the negatives instead of the positives.

In such instances, it is useful to **expand your positive second-hand references**. In this day and age, it is relatively easy to expand second-hand references, through books, magazines, television, the Internet, attending schools, seminars, e-mail correspondence, traveling, mentoring, and so forth. There are so many questions to ask to stimulate growth in this area, and they all center around helping you expand your set of references:

1. Who has already done this that can help you? How can you reach her? Did she write a book? Can you meet her in person? Who has worked with her?

2. How did your role model achieve his goal? What steps did he follow?

3. Who has achieved success in this particular area that has had a similar background as you? How could you learn what to do?

4. What magazines, books, articles, classes or groups might give you new insight?

5. What web sites are available to help you?

6. Where might you travel to help give you new insights, ideas and experiences?

7. How might joining this team / club / group help give you new ideas or references?

Challenging Limiting References

To possess a Winning Mind Set™, it is of paramount importance that you pay strict attention to your limiting references. Like weeds, they are easy to pull out when small. If they grow and multiply, they are that much tougher to eradicate. A table with only a few legs is easy to topple; one with many is quite solid and more difficult to take down. Consider the following phrases:

Everybody else can do ...

I *always* ...

Every time ...

No one ...

I could *never* / I'll *never* ...

I *can't* ...

If ever you find yourself talking to yourself (or others) in this way, pull out those weeds by asking these powerful questions:

Everybody else can do ... **Everybody? There isn't any person that can't do that?**

I always ... **I always? Has there ever been a time when I haven't done that?**

Every time ... **Every time? Was there ever a time that I...?**

No one ... **No one?**

I could never / I'll never ... **Never? Am I sure?**

I can't ... **Can't? Am I positive? Have I ever done it in the past, or something like it that can at least get me started?**

Don't stop there. Make sure there are no roots left in the soil. Fish around with some more questions to insure that you have wiped out that confidence-sapping thought:

- Everybody else can do ... **Everybody? There isn't any person that can't do that?** Well, not everybody else can do it, some people can't (weakened the reference – an opening). **Knowing that there are some people that can't, how does that change things?**
- I always ... **I always? Has there ever been a time when I haven't done that?** Yes, there has. **I actually have had success in this situation. So what would have to happen for me to be able to repeat that success here, now, in this situation?**
- Every time ... **Every time? Was there ever a time that I...?**

I guess there was. **I have been successful in the past. What made me successful then, and how might I use that to help me here, now?**

- No one ... **No one?** Well, maybe not no one. **So there is someone. And what would it take for me to ask that person for help?**

- I could never / I'll never ... **Never? Am I sure?** Well, maybe I could. **I have been able to do this in the past, haven't I? What would it take to make me feel confident in this situation?**

- I can't ... **Can't? Am I positive? Have I ever done it in the past?** A long time ago. **Okay, a long time ago, and even though it was a long time ago, some things you never forget, like riding a bike. It can be years and years since I have ridden a bike, yet I jump back on and my body has a way of remembering exactly what to do.**

Playing out the Consequences of Limiting Beliefs

Sometimes you may not have positive references in a certain area, or for whatever reason cannot or will not focus upon them, and so the questioning technique above isn't effective. In such cases it is often useful to switch to a different approach, one of playing out the negative consequences of your limiting belief. We human beings are always trying to avoid pain and to gain pleasure. Utilizing consequences can help you to shift what your ideas of pain and pleasure are.

For example, if you are trying to get yourself to take an action, say start an exercise and nutritional regimen in order to help you get to your ideal body weight and composition, yet you have struggled with this in the past and have never had any success. If you tried the techniques above and they didn't work for you (then), play out the consequences of your limiting belief:

I can never stick to an exercise and eating plan for more than a couple of weeks.

If you can't, then...
- How will you look and feel a year from now?
- How will that impact your energy level?
- How will that effect what you are willing to try or not try?
- What will you never do because you don't feel like you have the energy?
- How will that impact your relationships?
- How will that impact other areas of your life?

Often times, we don't like going into the future and seeing the consequences of these limiting beliefs. Why not? Because we don't like what we see. We want to continue to believe that it won't be so bad, and that we really don't have to change our behavior. By forcing yourself to venture into the future, you get associated to what your life will be like if you don't make a change now. It is even more powerful when you link this to your core values. We have an example of this in the Values section; if this isn't 100% clear now, don't worry. Once you go through the Values chapter it will become apparent how to utilize this technique.

Imagining Success

Imagination is more important than knowledge.

-ALBERT EINSTEIN

Someone once said, "The body will not achieve what the mind cannot conceive." Like Roger Bannister, there are instances in which there are no references for an achievement. Since it has never been done, no one has a personal reference for success in the area, and no one can look to others for second-hand references either. In these cases imagination must be used to create references that are as real as those that we actually experience. In addition, imagining future successes is also useful to supplant existing personal and second-hand references. In either case, the use of imagination is a powerful way to create and strengthen beliefs.

You may have heard about the following research experiment. A group of college students were selected at random, and divided into three groups. All three groups were asked to shoot a number of baskets from the foul line of a basketball court – free throws. Each group was scored and a baseline percentage was established for each group.

The first group was told to practice basketball free throws for an hour a day for two weeks. The second group was told to imagine shooting foul shots for the same amount of time, but not to actually do it. The third group was told just to come back in two weeks.

At the end of the two weeks, the researchers retested all three groups. The third group, the one that neither practiced nor mentally rehearsed, did not improve at all. The first group, the ones that actually practiced for an hour a day, and the second group, who mentally rehearsed practicing, both improved by virtually the same amount. Because the second group had some actual experience of shooting foul shots, they used that memory to mentally rehearse and imagine success.

The only place where your dreams become impossible is in your own thinking.

- ROBERT SCHULLER

Visualizing Success

Go get someone else to help you out on this next exercise. It's a simple yet great example of the power of mental rehearsal and visualizing success. A gentleman named Moshe Feldenkrais, an Israeli physicist and black belt in judo, developed it. It is an example of a technology he pioneered called "Psychophysical reeducation." Don't do this if you have back problems that would contraindicate such type of movement. In general, it should be appropriate for most people.

To do this, you need someone else to read this aloud to you:

Stand comfortably with your feet shoulder width apart. Extend your right pointer finger as you slowly raise your right arm to shoulder level. Keeping your arm straight and you finger pointing out, turn clockwise as far as you can comfortably without hurting yourself or straining, just as far as you can easily and note to where your finger ends up pointing.

Now turn back around so that you face straight ahead, and relax your arm so that it hangs by your side. Now, with your eyes closed, simply imagine that your right arm is coming up to your shoulder level, with your finger extending out. Don't actually do it, simply *imagine* that you are doing it. Now, imagine that you are turning clockwise again, just as you did before, but this time go a third further than you did before. Imagine that you can do that now, and it's easy, there is no strain or stress. Can you feel it?

Now, in your mind, turn back around so you are once again facing straight ahead, and let your arm drop back down so that it hangs comfortably by your side.

Once again, with your eyes still closed, imagine that you are raising your arm, with your finger extended, and this time go even further than before. It doesn't hurt at all, and it may seem a little bit odd to be able to go that far. Feel it, and once again, imagine that you turn back around so you are once again facing straight ahead, and let your arm drop back down so that it hangs comfortably by your side.

One last time, with your eyes still closed, imagine that you are raising your arm, with your finger extended out into space, and this time go even further than you have so far so that you go completely around, a full 360 degrees. It may seem weird that you can go that far, but you can without any strain or stress. Now once again, imagine that you turn back around so you are once again facing straight ahead, and let your arm drop back down so that it hangs comfortably by your side.

Great, now open your eyes. When I say to, I want you to actually turn around in a clockwise direction as far as you can comfortably, without stretching or straining and see how far you go.

What is interesting about this exercise is that most people

report going about a third farther than they did on their initial "real" attempt. Why? They always had the potential to go that far. They didn't do dozens of repetitions to get their blood flowing and raise their body temperature. They didn't stretch so that they could turn further. What they did was mentally rehearse going further in order to tap into a potential that was always there.

In terms of what you have learned, in the first repetition of this exercise, you had a certain potential for free movement which is set based on muscles, tendons, ligaments and bones. Based on that potential, you took some action. Based on that action you obtained a result. From that result you had a personal reference about your capability, which acted as a "leg" for a belief about how far you could turn without feeling strain or pain.

In the next three rounds, you still had the same potential, right? But, you visualized going further each time by mentally taking more action, which gave you an imagined reference for what was possible. This created a new belief, which allowed you to tap into more of your potential. When you did it again for real, these imagined references in fact allowed you to go to a place that had up until that point only been achieved in your mind. Your imagination paved the way for what your body could do.

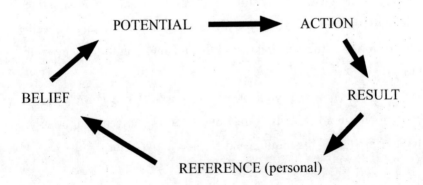

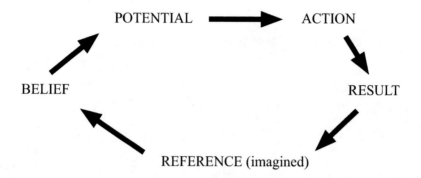

Now if your results in this simple exercise improved so much with just a few seconds of rehearsal, you might begin to wonder how much you can improve in other areas of your life if you really began to apply this idea.

Success Sensing

Different people imagine differently. Some utilize primarily visual senses, others kinesthetic, others auditory, others tactile, and still others (to a lesser extent) olfactory and gustatory. We often use the term *visualization,* but in truth it is more accurate to describe it as *success sensing,* utilizing whatever modes make the most sense for you. Your goal is to imagine the future as vividly as possible. After all, most people have no trouble imagining the worst, so that proves they are good at imagining. You just need to get really good at imagining more positive experiences. The more senses that are involved the better, because multiple modalities make more neural connections in the brain than will one single modality.

So as you visualize success, get all of your senses involved. What will it look like? How will it sound? What will it feel like? Get your sense of taste and smell involved too. We will share more exercises involving visualization in future chapters.

Beliefs
Key Points to Remember

1) The three basic concepts of beliefs are:

      1) Categories

      2) Structure (References)

      3) Effects

2) The two major categories of beliefs are:

      1) If/Then Beliefs

      2) Categorical Beliefs

3) There are three kinds of references that support our beliefs.

      1) Our Personal References

      2) Our Second-hand References

      3) Our Imagined References

4) The effects of a belief either empower us or limit us in some way.

5) Some of our beliefs may be at odds with each other sending us conflicting messages.

6) Our beliefs are based on the references that we choose to focus on.

7) Four methods to change limiting beliefs are:

1) Reinforcing and expanding our positive personal and second-hand references.

2) Challenging our limiting references.

3) Playing out the consequences of our limiting beliefs.

4) Imagining success by using the power of our imagined references.

On the day before EPCOT was set to open in Disney World, Roy Disney was overlooking the tremendous accomplishment with another Disney executive. The other gentleman remarked, "It's too bad Walt wasn't here to see this," referring to the fact that Walt Disney had passed away prior to the center's completion. Roy smiled and replied, "He saw it first, and that's why we are seeing it."

Chapter Three

Emotions

'While we may not be able to control all that happens to us,
we can control what happens inside us.'

- BENJAMIN FRANKLIN

Have you ever been "in the zone"? Can you remember a specific time where everything seemed to be working together, where you felt totally confident and unstoppable? Go back there now, and relive that experience in as much detail as possible. Picture everything that you could see back then, hear all the sounds that you heard, feel all of the sensations you felt.

How were you holding your body when you felt absolutely confident and unstoppable? How were you breathing? What were you picturing? How were you talking to yourself? What did your body feel like?

If you were to get even more specific and more associated to that positive memory, you could probably identify a certain posture, a certain way of breathing, a certain way you moved your body, and even a certain way of focusing to create this emotional state of being in the zone, of confidence and feeling unstoppable.

Beliefs determine how we feel and what we do, yet our emotions have a huge impact on which references we tend to focus upon, and which corresponding beliefs seem to be most real to us. In certain emotional states, we tend to think in a positive manner and focus on more empowering beliefs, experiences and references. In other emotional states, however, we tend to focus on more disempowering beliefs, experiences and references. One critical component to a Winning Mind Set™ is to determine how to get yourself in the right frame of mind (emotional state) to do what you want and need to do.

In this chapter you'll learn how to better understand and manage your emotions on a consistent basis in order to bring out the best in you. After all, what we will do in any given moment depends not as much on our ability, as on our state of mind.

What we will do in any given moment depends not as much on our ability as on our state of mind.

The Fear Factor by Kevin Seaman

While coaching the Professional Kite boarders at the 2005 World Cup in Cabarete, Dominican Republic, one of the athletes was worried about the feelings he experienced in his stomach prior to competition. His belief was that the butterflies were signaling fear, and that as a result he wouldn't perform well. I explained that this was totally normal, and that this was actually his body's way of preparing him for combat, or for a great challenge, that this was a powerful force that he could use to his advantage, and not something he should fear.

Once he heard that, he changed his mindset almost instantly. You could see the corresponding change in his body too. He went from timid to confident in a matter of a few seconds. I further explained to him how important this process was, and how the adrenaline that accompanies it is key to his success, that if he did not feel this, then we would have some concern.

During the competition he performed without hesitation, nailing nearly every move with incredible agility. Later on he told me that the advice I gave him helped him perform the best he had ever in competition.

Emotions Awareness Exercise

List below four positive emotions you experience on an ongoing basis.

1)

2)

3)

4)

Take a moment and think about what it takes or what you have to do in order to experience that emotion. What pattern or ritual, in other words, do you run emotionally and physically in both your mind and body previous to that experience?

1)

2)

3)

4)

List below four negative emotions you experience on a regular basis.

1)

2)

3)

4)

Take a moment and think about what it takes or what you have to do in order to experience these negative emotions. What ritual, in other words, do you run emotionally and physically in both your mind and body previous to each experience?

1)

2)

3)

4)

There are six major techniques we will share to help you understand and direct your emotions more consistently and effectively:

1. Physiology
2. Breathing
3. Reframing
4. Questions
5. Figures of Speech
6. Words

Physiology of Success

The way you stand, how you present yourself physically will almost instantaneously transform your own self-confidence and emotional content, while altering the way others respond to you as well! We have all seen the posture of confidence, tenacity, and fear. If a team wants to intimidate you physically and you let them, they've WON.

-MIA HAMM
WORLD CUP SOCCER CHAMPION

Anthony Robbins is fond of saying, "Motion creates emotion." He contends, quite correctly, that one of the quickest ways to change how you feel is to change how you use your body. Changing the way you move, gesture, sit, stand and breathe instantly changes how you feel.

When you are tired and need to re-energize, what do you do? You stand up, breathe deeply, stretch, or take a walk. You initiate some kind of movement to alter how you feel; your *motion* alters your *emotion*.

What about exercising? Have you ever had those days where you were dragging, perhaps wondering why you do this to yourself? But what happened after you warmed up? Chances are you began to feel awake and alive. By the end of your training you probably felt fantastic; and by the way, if you consistently exercise, it is almost a guarantee that this is the feeling you will tend to focus upon when you think about working out, not the dragging, dreading feeling. Remember, when we introduced beliefs and the references we choose to focus upon? Again, you radically changed the way you used your body, which resulted in experiencing a dramatically different emotional state.

When we remain in a certain physiology for a period of time, we tend to stay in the same emotional state as well. Moreover, there are certain physiologies for certain emotional states. Think about it. If we asked you to describe someone who was totally depressed, you could do it, couldn't you? Isn't there a body language or physiology for depression? Where would this person's head be? Up or hanging down? Hanging down, probably. What about this person's breathing, full and deep, or weak and shallow? Weak and shallow, most likely. Would their face be smiling and animated? Probably not, most likely it would be slack and expressionless. Would their movements and gestures be expansive and quick, or slow and minimal? Their gestures, if they had any at all, would probably be slow and minimal.

Now, how do you know this? Because you've "been there and done that." We've all had days when just getting out of bed seemed like a chore.

Motion creates emotion.

-ANTHONY ROBBINS

On the other hand, we also know that doing something as simple as lifting our head up, putting our shoulders back, breathing fully and smiling tend to make us feel more energized, awake and alive. There have even been studies in which patients in mental health institutions were instructed to put a pen in their teeth, smile and look up at the ceiling for twenty minutes a day. As ridiculous and simplistic as that may seem, the study actually found that many of these patients reduced the amount of medication they needed to take by half.

It is essential to understand that some of the most powerful chemicals around are in our bodies. Our bodies' natural opiates, for example, are much more powerful in comparable amounts than the drug opium. Changing the way we use our bodies significantly alters and affects our biochemical processes. Learning to be aware of our physiology and how it affects our performance is an important step in controlling our outcome.

Change your mind, change your body
Change your body and you change your mind!

How can you use this knowledge of physiology to engender a Winning Mind Set™? Let's see how Jim used this knowledge to help his daughter Rachel approach a challenge.

—⌒🦋⌒—

Jim's Winning Mind Set™ Example
– A Backwards Roll

I came home one day only to find my usually cheerful wife in a foul mood. "Go talk to Rachel," she said, meaning our daughter who was then seven years old.

"What's up?" I asked.

"She wants to quit dancing, and she's all in a snit." I could see she wasn't the only one. I went upstairs to Rachel's room to find her face down on her bed, surrounded by a sea of stuffed animals. "Hi, Bean. Hey, could you come upstairs with me for a minute?" **(1)** She slowly lifted her head, and grudgingly got up and followed me into my room. She sat on the edge of the bed, her chin tucked into her chest, a big frown on her usually smiling face. I sat down next to her in a similar position. "So, Mommy said that something was bothering you?"

"I hate dance," she moaned. This from a girl who absolutely loved to dance, something she had been doing since she was three.

"Wow, okay. It seems like you have liked dance in the past, what changed?"

"Everybody else can do a backwards roll except me!" she blurted.

"I see. Everybody?" I inquired.

"Well, not everybody, but almost everybody, and I can't even do one, and I don't want to go back there."

"Okay, I could see how it would be hard to go back to a place like that." I paused for a moment. "How does it feel to ride a two-wheeler?"

"What?"

"A two-wheeler. How does it feel to be able to ride a two-wheeler instead of a bike with training wheels?"

She shrugged. "Okay."

"What happened when we took off your training wheels and you began to learn to ride without them?"

She pondered that question for a moment. "I fell."

"Oh, how did that feel?"

Another shrug. "Not great."

"Not great," I replied. "But what made you keep going? How come you didn't quit?"

A third shrug. "I don't know, I guess I just wanted to do it."

"Oh, you just wanted to do it. So you kept trying and trying, even if it didn't feel great and you didn't do it perfectly yet, because it was important to you."

"Yeah," she said, a tiny smile just beginning to break through the pouted lips.

"So what would happen if, because you were so frustrated as you learned to do something that you never kept trying, that you never learned to do something new, and you were a big seven year old with training wheels? How would that be to be riding a baby bike with training wheels now?"

"Not good," she answered.

"Not good. So how did you get through that frustrating period learning to ride your bike? How did you manage to do that?"

"I just did it. I wanted to do it enough that I kept trying until I got it."

"And you did get it, right? She nodded her head. "What would happen if, because you are a little frustrated as you learn to do something new called a backwards roll, that you stopped? And you never went back to dance when it is something you really like to do, and everyone else kept getting better and better, just because you were a little frustrated?"

"I would feel bad."

"You would feel bad if you stopped, I see. Well, what would happen if you absolutely knew you could do a backwards roll now. What would be the look on your face?" **(2)** I said as I lifted my shoulders and head up just a bit.

Rachel tried hard not to smile. "It would be happy."

"And what would that look like?" I continued, my voice becoming louder, faster, and more animated.

"Like this," she said breaking into a grin.

"Great!" I smiled along with her as I straightened up even more. "And what about your shoulders? Where would they be?" **(3)**

"Here," she said as she straightened up even more.

"That's right, and how would you be breathing right now if you absolutely knew you could do a backwards roll now?" **(4)**

She took a deep breath, and sprung off the bed. "Watch me!" She squatted down on the floor, and rolled backwards. About halfway through she tumbled to the side. "Wait. I know I can do it," she chirped, and readied herself once again. This time she executed a perfect backwards roll. She stood up beaming with a smile from ear-to-ear. "I did it!" she shouted, and ran to me for a hug.

"That's great," I said as I hugged her to me. "I knew you could. So," I said as she let go, "how do you feel about dance now?"

"I love it!"

Let's investigate the *Backwards Roll* example to see how Jim used the power of changing one's physiology with Rachel.

(1) He asked her to follow him to another room. Why not talk there? To get her to move!

(2) He asked her what her face would look like if she knew she could do a backwards roll.

(3) He asked to show him what her shoulders would be like and how she would be sitting if she were confident.

(4) He asked her to breathe the way she would breathe if she were totally confident.

By asking Rachel to act as if she were already confident in this ability, and imagine what she would experience in her body, she was basically getting into her "physiology of success". She remembered previous experiences of success, and put herself into a physiology that matched that feeling. From that physiology of success, she was able to execute a movement that she was always capable of, save the negative thinking and physiology.

Your outer world is a direct reflection of your inner world.

Jim once worked with an executive, who was in a good mood 95% of the time, and he was almost always whistling when he walked. Jim said that he was never sure if he was whistling because he was happy, or if he was happy because he whistled.

The point here is that the way we think affects our emotions, which affects our bodies. And the way we use our bodies affects the way we think and feel. It's a chicken and egg phenomenon. There is a reciprocal relationship and impact. As Rachel changed her thoughts, her body started to change, and as she started to change her physiology, her thoughts began to change.

Remember from the section on beliefs that we have personal, second-hand and imagined references. Well, the same three categories apply to physiologies of success as well; by the way, "success" in this context means the physiology that helps to produce an emotional state that best suits the requirements of the situation. One can have a *personal reference* of a state such as confidence, decisiveness, or patience. One can also *role model* someone else who exhibits these characteristics *(second-hand references)*, and one can *imagine* what it would be like to be in that type of state *(imagined reference)* and your body will begin to adapt those characteristics.

Winning Mind Set™ Exercise - Pick a state, any state!

Determine the emotional state you want to be in. It can be an active state, such as confident, energized, motivated, juiced, jazzed, amped up, or "on fire!" It can also be a more passive state, such as patient, compassionate, pensive, or relaxed. It's probably a good idea to try at least one of each.

Get into that state as completely as you can by using your personal references. Go back to a specific time that you felt that way, recalling the situation in as much detail as possible. Pay attention to how you used your physiology – what you did with your head, your shoulders, how much you moved, expressions, and so on.

Next, try getting into that state using second hand references, or a role model. How would your role model act if he or she were totally confident, patient, motivated, or compassionate? Try to mimic his or her movements as fully as you can.

Lastly, try getting into your desired state while using **your imagined references**. That is, imagine yourself in a situation where you are in that state. As you imagine it more vividly, notice what is happening to your physiology.

You may have different results depending on the emotional state you are targeting. You might be excellent at getting into a state of confidence by focusing on personal references, but may do better at being patient when thinking of a role model, or vice versa.

Breathing

Breathing may be the master function of the body,
affecting all others.

- DR. ANDREW WEIL

How long can you go without eating? Although some people feel like they are going to "starve" if they don't eat every couple of hours, the truth is that we can go a long time without eating; weeks, maybe even as long as a month. What about without drinking? Only a few days at most, right? What about breathing? We can only last a matter of seconds or minutes without breathing, so it would make sense that how we breathe would have an enormous effect on how we feel.

The average adult breathes at a rate of sixteen to twenty breaths per minute. When it slows down to eight per minute, the brain wave patterns alter so that you feel relaxed yet alert; you have an increased mental awareness. When it gets down to four breaths per minute, inhaling and exhaling being one cycle, then the emotional state one experiences is one of extreme calm, improved visual clarity, heightened sensitivity in the body, and expanded feelings of awareness. When it gets down to one per minute or less, there is an optimization of the two hemispheres of the brain, resulting in a significant lessening of fear, worry, and anxiety, and an increased reliance on intuition. It is a state of absolute bliss; a meditative, detached state, and it also boosts your immune system.

With these slower rates of breathing, your reaction to your thoughts changes significantly. Your thoughts will still come, but your response to those thoughts changes dramatically. For instance, at a normal rate of breathing, you may have a thought, and with that a corresponding bodily reaction to that thought. You may picture someone you don't like and think, "I can't stand her," and your insides tighten and your face flushes. Your heartbeat quickens and adrenaline releases into your bloodstream.

At a slower rate of breathing, you have the same thought about that person. But now your reaction is different. You don't get angry. You simply notice your thought as if you are watching a movie about someone else. You are detached from your feeling. "Oh, it's that person, again. What an odd style she has." But you will have a reduced bodily reaction or no perceptible reaction whatsoever.

Dr. Robert Fried, in his research article *The Psychology and*

Physiology of Breathing, <u>Behavioral Medicine, Clinical Psychology, and Psychiatry</u>, 1993, reported that his exhaustive review of the available literature at the time led him to conclude that normal breathing has been overlooked or underemphasized by much of the medical community. His studies revealed that shallow breathing, hyperventilation and other abnormal breathing patterns were a complication of or causal factor in 50 to 70 percent of medical complaints. He found that by providing training in proper breathing, he could alleviate a range of common maladies, including emotional problems and circulatory difficulties.

Gurucharan Singh Khalsa, Ph.D., and Yogi Bhajan, Ph.D., have produced a book and accompanying audiotape program called **Breathwalk: Breathing Your Way to a Revitalized Body, Mind, and Spirit.** In the book, the authors share a series of sixteen combined breathing and walking exercises that are geared specifically toward helping create very specific emotional states in the practitioner such as openness, learning, creativity, integrity, focus, mental clarity, motivation, receptiveness, connection, calmness, and energy. They teach that changing our breathing affects our autonomic nervous system, the one that automatically governs basic processes like heart rate and blood pressure, and affects other physiologic processes such as digestion, glandular secretions and certain nervous system functions. By changing our breathing, we can stimulate our brain, particularly the hypothalamus, to secrete hormones that affect our moods; by consciously doing so, we can create any emotion that we desire.

In this very breath that we take now lies the secret that all great teachers try to tell us.

- PETER MATTHIESSEN

69

Altering your breathing, either through a method such as Breathwalk, or through exercising, meditation, or simple attention, can produce significant and rapid shifts in people's emotions. These methods may seem so simple to people; however many times the simple methods are the most effective, especially as a foundation for other approaches.

Winning Mind Set™ Breathing Awareness Exercise

Take a few moments to try out various breathing patterns. For the first two minutes, just breathe normally, counting the number of complete breaths per minute (inhalation and exhalation is one complete breath). Breathe in and out through your nose if you can. At the end of that time, simply jot down the number of breaths per minute, and also a few words to describe what you are thinking about, along with the emotion that best describes how you feel:

Normal breathing: _____ x per minute. I was thinking about ....I would best describe my emotion as...

Next, try to make your breathing more deep, but quicker and more forceful in a way that is comfortable for you, but don't overdo it – do what is right for you. Breathe in through your nose, and out through your mouth, for two minutes. Make sure your belly is moving in and out as you breathe so that you engage the entire lungs. At the end of that time, simply jot down the number of breaths per minute, and also a few words to describe what you are thinking about, along with the emotion that best describes how you feel:

Forceful breathing: _____ x per minute. I was thinking about ....
I would best describe my emotion as...

Now, try slowing down your breath. Breathe in through your nose fully and completely, making sure that your belly is going out as you inhale. Then slowly exhale through your nose, letting your belly sink in as you do so. Do this for two minutes. At the end of that time, simply jot down the number of breaths per minute, and also a few words to describe what you are thinking about, along with the emotion that best describes how you feel:

Relaxed breathing: _____ x per minute. I was thinking about ....I would best describe my emotion as...

How to use this: Begin the habit of deep, diaphragmatic breathing immediately. This is the most practical and effective method for healthy breathing. Always try to breathe deeply and slowly. Your homework (yes, homework) is to take note of your breathing while engaging in physical activities and while at rest. Make a conscious effort to breathe from your diaphragm whenever possible throughout the week. When you feel yourself too relaxed and need to become active, try increasing your rate of breaths per minute. If you want to relax, slow your breathing. You will control your energy, by controlling your breathing. It's that profoundly simple. Always breathe deep, you will see and feel the difference when you do.

Reframing

When Goliath came against the Isrealites,
the soldiers all thought, "He's so big we can never kill him."
But David looked at the same giant and thought,
"He's so big, I can't miss him."
— DALE TURNER

Our emotions are dramatically affected by the meaning we give to our experiences, and the meaning we give to any experience is shaped by the lens or filter through which we perceive it. The quote from Dale Turner is a wonderful example of the power of reframing. Whereas the other soldiers all were afraid of Goliath's mammoth presence, David saw the situation in another, entirely different way. His frame of reference enabled him to feel powerful instead of petrified.

Reframing is an invaluable tool for creating a Winning Mind Set™. It gives you the opportunity to see things in different, more empowering perspectives. For example, a woman was speaking with Jim, lamenting about how undisciplined she was. "I start swimming, and go a few times, then I don't go for a week or two because I get so busy. I'm so undisciplined, and then when I go back it is as if I never went at all. It's like starting over anew each time."

Jim reframed her experience for her. "You know, I would say that requires an extraordinary amount of discipline to keep going back and starting new. Once you are in shape, it's easy to keep it up. But for you going back each time, feeling out of breath and tired, yet continuing to go back anyway, I'd say that you possess a lot of discipline."

So what does such a reframing do? Well, if she continued to languish in her state of self-flagellation about how undisciplined she was for not swimming consistently, do you think she would be more or less apt to want to go? Probably less likely to want to go swimming. But, if she felt a sense of pride in her continued ability to keep repeating the most difficult part of exercising, the beginning, she would feel better about swimming. Potentially, if she realized that she had enough discipline to keep doing the hardest part, she might transfer that new identity of being a self-disciplined person to enable her to swim on a more consistent basis.

How we feel about something and what we do is determined by the meaning we give to that situation.

That particular reframing reminds us of research that has been done with self-rated pessimists and optimists. Both groups of people were given a series of tasks to perform which could be easily measured. When they completed the work, both groups were scored, and the researchers found that both performed equally, completing approximately 75% of the tasks correctly. When asked how they thought they did on the various tasks, the pessimists were much more accurate. The optimists were off by a much higher degree, and consistently rated themselves as doing better than they actually did.

What we found interesting, though, is that when asked if they would like to try again to improve their scores, the optimists were much more likely to want to try again. Because they thought they did better, they were more motivated to keep going. The pessimists, on the other hand, felt that they hadn't done that well (from their frame of mind), and were much less motivated to repeat the task. One could surmise from such research that if an individual believes she has done well (like being disciplined enough to keep going through the start-up phase of exercise), then she is more inclined to want to continue.

How, then, can you reframe a situation? Easy.

All that you have to do is ask different questions. Consider the following:

- How might this be seen in a positive way?

- How can I use this constructively?
- What is actually good about this that I may be overlooking?
- In what ways does this get me closer to my goal?
- What did I learn from this that I could use in the future?
- What did I learn about myself?
- What lesson can I take from this?
- How will this experience make me better?

I am not discouraged,
because every wrong attempt discarded
is another step forward.
-THOMAS A. EDISON

Here's a short list of a few people that once "failed":

- The game Monopoly was originally rejected for containing 52 fundamental errors. Today the game is so successful that Parker Brothers prints more than $60 billion of Monopoly money each year.
- Michael Jordan was cut from his High School Basketball Team for his lack of talent.
- Babe Ruth struck out 1,330 times (but he also hit 714 home runs)
- Steven Spielberg dropped out of high school in his sophomore year. He was persuaded to come back and placed in a learning disabled class. He lasted a month.
- Beethoven's music teacher once told him that as a composer, he was hopeless.
- Winston Churchill failed the 6th grade.

- John Creasy, the English novelist who wrote 564 books, was rejected 753 times before he became established.
- Charles Darwin's father told him he would amount to nothing and would be a disgrace to himself and his family.
- Walt Disney was fired by the editor of a newspaper because Disney had "no good ideas".
- When Thomas Edison was a boy his teacher told him he was too stupid to learn anything.

The approach used by Thomas Edison offers a classic example of reframing. It took him more than 10,000 attempts to invent the incandescent light bulb. When others chided him for failing so many times, and asked when he was going to give up his crazy idea, he was reported to have said, "I didn't fail, I just figured out another way *not* to invent the light bulb." He reframed what others saw as failure into a new distinction. He saw it as gaining more knowledge because he now knew one more approach that did not work, and so he could save time and effort by avoiding going in that particular direction. Because his reframing made him feel empowered and excited, he persevered. Had he been discouraged because he had failed yet again, chances are high that he would not have had the motivation to continue.

Many successful salespeople know that their success comes down to ratios, that they receive a certain number of "no's" for every "yes". To them, every no is one step closer to a yes.

The challenge that many have is that they look into the future and project their current failure. So instead of feeling down only about their current result, they project it to include all future results. An internal dialogue might go something like this: "If I messed up here, and I've done it before, I'll probably do it later as well, and I can't believe I keep doing this. I'll never get any better, I don't even know why I bother..."

One objective of reframing is to limit the emotion of "failure", which may include feelings of guilt, frustration, apprehension, and dejection, to the present experience only so that this negative emotion is not projected into the future. The other objective is to change the meaning of the current experience from a negative, disempowering one, into a positive, empowering one; from a feeling of "I can't believe I screwed up so badly," to "I just learned what not to do in that situation." Using reframing to focus and direct your emotions into positive change creates a Winning Mind Set™ and motivates you to continue to strive towards reaching your goals.

The way you interpret events to yourself determines your emotional responses to those events

---

Consider the following scenario

Have you ever noticed how the same thing can happen to three or more people and affect all of them differently? If, for example, we're faced with a challenge, such as being late for a meeting or appointment then suddenly having car trouble. To one person this may be difficult to handle, their self-communication may go something like this: "Why does this <u>always</u> happen to me? That piece of junk! Why did I buy that stupid thing in the first place? I never should have let him talk me into this meeting! Nothing ever goes right! I've had it! # * Ø # * * !!! (an extremely negative and very self-convincing internal dialog). Even worse, this person will continue to mull it over and over in his mind, reliving it for a good part of the day. On top of that, he will tell everyone how upset he is, allowing this minor setback to control his focus, mood and productivity for the rest of the day, possibly affecting their entire week. Does this seem familiar? Do you know anyone like this?

Some of us tend to blame other people or things when our expectations aren't met. This type of blaming shifts the responsibility somewhere else. The problem with shifting "blame" is it makes you feel powerless over your life, since it is contingent on the actions and behavior of others, or conditions which you can't control.

Another person may have the exact same thing happen, yet experiences the same event in a very different way. As they reflect on their problem they may talk to themselves something like this: "Oh shoot! Now what am I going to do? I probably should have given myself more time. This is embarrassing. I'll never make it on time now! I really blew it!" His thoughts are not quite as angry, although very negative and conclusively self-defeating. Think about these two approaches--when they ask negative questions, their minds search for negative answers! Like them, many of us are guilty of focusing 90% of our thoughts on our problem and only 10% on solutions. Both of these individuals focused so adamantly on their problem that it overwhelmed any possibility for a solution. When you stop blaming yourself and others, you begin to gain a better sense of control over your problem. Now let's look at the same situation from a more "solution-oriented" approach: "Uh...oh, something is wrong with the car? I've got plenty of gas. I better take a look under the hood. Well, I can't see anything obvious. I think I'll leave a note on the windshield and get to a phone. Maybe we can reschedule the appointment? Hi John, I'm on my way however I ran into a little problem. My car's not cooperating, can we reschedule? Really, great! Tomorrow same time. See you then, thanks John!"

What a difference between the last approach and the first two thought patterns! When you stop blaming yourself and others, you will begin to gain a better sense of control over your problem. Did you know that the quality of your life is a direct result of the quality of your communication, both internally (with yourself) and externally (with others)? You see, in life it's not what happens to us, but how we interpret it that gives it meaning. It's not life, but how you represent life that determines the way you feel. Actually we don't experience reality; we experience our representation of reality. And, just how do we represent our thoughts? We "re-present" our thoughts through the words we use. In fact, one of the most powerful principles of controlling our attitude is by controlling our thoughts through the words we use. For example, is it a *catastrophe* or a *problem*? Is it a *disaster* or a *challenge*? When you seek to de-amplify your problem, you will find it easier to take control of that problem and work towards a solution.

Although we have little control over the stress we face in our lives, what we *can* control is how well we respond to these problems. We realize we can limit our risk factors, but we cannot control how or when we may be challenged. We can, however, control how we respond. People who are highly skilled at problem solving possess the ability to respond quickly and effectively when faced with a challenge or problem. They demonstrate high levels of "response-ability" on a daily basis. Contrast this with most people's inability to control their emotional responses. Many people start with the belief that they are victims – that things happen *to* them and that things are beyond their control. People who feel this way are said to operate from an external locus of control. They feel that their lives are controlled by their environment, their bosses, the government and other controlling forces outside of themselves. They want others to change, they want the world to change, but they themselves don't want to change. People with this outlook tend to be average to below average achievers.

On the other hand, people who feel that they are in control of their lives take control. They believe that if they are to succeed, it is up to them to make it happen. These individuals possess an internal locus of control. They take full responsibility for their actions or inaction. People with an internal locus of control tend to be low stress, high performance personalities.

The bottom line is you feel good about yourself to the degree that you feel that you are in control of your own life, and research has shown that a "sense of control" is absolutely essential in order for you to perform at your best. This is a core belief of the Winning Mind Set™.

So whatever happens to you in life, take responsibility for your actions (responses) and learn from the outcome. If you do not like what has happened, take control toward changing the outcome. You will have bad days; times when you start to lose it. When you do, don't worry. Just try to be more conscious and view it as a learning opportunity. Remember, life is a process. Mark Twain once said, "I have been through some terrible things in my life, some of which actually happened."

Always look at what you have left.
Never look at what you have lost.
-ROBERT SCHULLER

It's All About Perspective!

What you say to yourself and others (the quality of your internal and external communication) has a lot to do with your representation of any given event. We have seen athletes lose, fail a shot, make an error or perform poorly, and talk about the event or beat themselves up for days.

Now, think about it, if something bad happens to you, do you review it your mind over and over, talking to other people, and telling them how awful it was? If so, we have a question for you: Did you experience this event once, or over and over? Wasn't once enough? Now remember, your subconscious thought process does not actually distinguish between thinking about something and the actual event. It is in fact considered real either way. This is one of the qualities of visualization, so utilize it in a positive way. Focusing on your problems creates a ripple effect, magnifying the experience in your mind. Focus on your solutions, not your problems. Solution oriented individuals learn from these experiences, rather than focus on them. The things you can do something about, put your heart into solving or resolving. The things you can't do anything about, let go of. Focus on what you want, not what you don't want. Be solution oriented and succeed more and more at everything you do.

Ultimately, success is not measured by first place prizes.
It's measured by the road we have traveled,
how you dealt with the challenges
and stumbling blocks you encountered along the way.

-NICOLE HAISLETT
THREE TIME OLYMPIC GOLD MEDALIST IN SWIMMING

Winning Mind Set Three Chair Exercise

One way to get good at reframing is to try the following exercise that helps you to see a single situation from three different perspectives. This exercise also teaches that your emotional reaction to any situation will be tied to the meaning you give to it, and that you actually have a tremendous amount of freedom in determining what anything means.

To do this exercise, set up three different chairs. You are to tell the same story from these three different "chairs", or perspectives. While sitting in the first chair, tell the story as a sad or disappointing story, and really focus on all the aspects of the story that could be considered disappointing or sad.

In the next chair, tell the story as a happy or positive one, and to focus on the elements of the story that are positive or happy.

Finally, sitting in the third chair, tell the story as a motivational one, a tale that would inspire others. While you may have difficulty telling the story from three different perspectives, give it a try, and make sure that the story doesn't start out one way, such as positive, and devolve into a depressing story. The goal here is to help you realize that there are always many ways to look at a situation, and the way you view a situation shapes how you will feel about it. It is like looking through a particular type of filter, your emotions will change according to which filter you are viewing the subject through.

When finished, jot down what you have learned, and how you expect to apply it in the future.

Questions

Always the beautiful answer who asks a more beautiful question.

-E. E. CUMMINGS

You Get What You Ask For

You get into a cab and the driver asks, "Where you going?" At that point you start telling him where you want to go. Then as he takes off you start giving him various conflicting directions sending him to locations totally unrelated to where you first asked him to go. Sounds ridiculous, doesn't it?

Yet many times we do the same exact things to ourselves. Instead of telling ourselves what we are going to do or what we want, we tell ourselves what we don't want. When we do consulting work with athletes we always start out asking them what they want. We're amazed at how often they will then tell us what they don't want.
Did you know, that humans have the most amazing built in homing device available, that there is only one other creature that has a goal seeking homing device that is as sophisticated and accurate as the one human beings posses? The homing pigeon is the only other being in the animal kingdom that even comes close. Did you also know that research has shown that people talk to themselves nearly 50,000 times per day? In fact, you're talking to yourself right now. You're probably saying, "That's amazing! I didn't know that." So, how can we use this?

What we say to ourselves prior or during any situation that demands a high level of performance, is a major key to the success or failure of that performance. Our emotional content absolutely affects us on a physical, as well as a on a psychological level. This is due to the fact that your outer world is a direct reflection of your inner world.

You will most probably agree that your body is physical and your ability and skill are also physical. Your emotions are biochemical in nature and are also physical. As an extension, your thoughts, self-talk and inner visions or visualizations are electrochemical events and also are therefore physical in nature. Initially and accumulatively your thoughts absolutely affect your performance in everything you do. In athletic competition, your thoughts and feelings are physical and are just as fundamentally important as your ability and skill. Now this is the deal, everything counts! What we think, what we say to ourselves, and others, and what we visualize is emotionalized, and in turn affects our overall emotional state. Whatever you think about most of the time becomes your reality.

Our emotions vividly affect our physiology, both outwardly and inwardly. Let's look at what occurs when you're angry. Your heart races, your blood pressure increases, you may begin to shake, your temperature may elevate, and you may even notice a distinctly acidic taste in your mouth. Negative emotions have long been associated with acid production in the human body. Is this just psychological, or is it physiological as well?

How about when you're sad? What happens? Your eyes water and tears develop, your pulse rate changes, you experience a flush of heat rush through your body, you begin to feel weak, almost drained. OK, now is this physical or just psychological? All of us can remember that incredible rush of energy and excitement that surges through or body when we are happy, the feeling of euphoria and physical pleasure when falling in love. The Winning Mind Set™ helps us become aware of how our emotional content absolutely affects us on a physical, as well as a on a psychological level in everything we do.

If you don't like the answer, ask a better question.

Our minds are formulated to seek exactly what we ask ourselves for. If you ask yourself, why can't I do this? Your mind will find information to support all the different reasons why you in fact, can't do it. If asked, why can't I lose weight? Your mind will support your conviction as to why that is as well. The profound reality is, we get what we ask for. Instead of, what's the matter with me? A better question would be, how can I improve these circumstances or how would someone else approach this, modeling someone you hold in high regard as a problem solver in that field or area?

Questions are extremely powerful tools for changing our mindsets. As we saw in the previous chapter on Beliefs, questions can do three things. They can *change what we focus on*, they can *change what we delete*, and they can *give us access to different resources* (who, what, where, how, when) to help achieve our desired ends. Questions can also help gain access to feelings or *emotional states* very quickly, and as such, you will want to become adept at asking excellent ones.

In this section on **Emotions**, we will look at four types of questions:

1. State-Inducing Questions
2. Double Binds
3. Possibility Thinking Questions
4. Problem Solving Questions

The first type of question is one that helps us get into specific emotional states. This type is called *State-Inducing Questions*, and we learned a lot of these from working with Anthony Robbins. You will want to become excellent at asking questions that help you quickly get into empowering states. These states can run the gamut of emotions, from confidence to patience, from understanding to decisiveness, from sensitivity to motivation, and just about every other feeling in between. Determine which emotions are most important to you, and design questions to help you quickly access those states.

In addition, the way you ask these questions is key. If you ask a kid, "What did you do in school today?" invariably they will say "Nothing". By the way, we have asked that same question to seminar participants in the United States, Europe and Asia, and everyone said that their kids would say the same thing – nothing!

Ask a better quality of question. Instead of "What did you do today in school" ask "What was the best thing you did in school today?" or "What was the most exciting part of school today?" or "What did you learn that interested you the most today?" and you will get a better quality answer. Ask a lousy question, you'll probably end up getting a lousy answer. Ask an insightful question, you'll most likely end up with an answer that gives you a new level of understanding. Ask a State-Inducing Question, and you will go into that emotional state in order to answer.

There is one caveat to the last statement, however. Sometimes we can answer such questions without truly entering that emotional state. For instance, you can ask yourself the question, "What am I truly grateful for in my life?" and can rattle off a list of responses by rote, but not really feel that state of gratitude. In such cases, you may find it quite helpful to use a follow-up question, such as "What about those things makes me feel that way?" to insure that you are fully experiencing the given emotion and not simply answering intellectually.

It is through questions that we grow, develop and improve. Questions shape our lives.

State-Inducing Questions

- What am I really *happy* about in my life right now? What about _____ makes me *feel happy*?
- What aspects of my performance am I *most pleased* with? What about _____ makes me *feel that way*?
- What is the *best thing* that happened to me today? What made it so *special*?
- What in my future am I *most excited* about? What about _____ makes me *feel excited*?
- What accomplishments am I *most proud* of? What about that accomplishment makes me *feel proud*?
- What have I *accomplished* in my life that, when I first thought of it, I never believed I could pull it off? What does having that reference of knowing that I can accomplish something despite difficult odds give you?
- Considering everything that I have in I life, what am I most *grateful* for? What about _____ makes me *feel grateful*?
- In what areas do I *feel most confident*? What makes me *feel so confident* in that situation?
- In what situations do I find yourself the most *patient*? How do I approach those situations to help me to *feel patient*?
- Who in my life *means the most* to me? What makes them so *special*?
- Who in my life *loves me*? How does that make me *feel to be loved* like that?
- In what types of situations do I *feel most relaxed*? What about those situations do I *find relaxing*?

Winning Mind Set™ State inducing Questions Exercise

Answer these State-Inducing Questions about yourself

What am I really happy about in my life right now? What about _____ makes me feel happy?

What aspects of my performance am I most pleased with? What about _____ makes me feel that way?

What is the best thing that happened to me today? What made it so special?

What in my future am I most excited about? What about_____ makes me feel excited?

What accomplishments am I most proud of? What about that accomplishment makes me feel proud?

What have I accomplished in my life that, when I first thought of it, I never believed I could pull it off? What does having that reference of knowing that I can accomplish something despite difficult odds give you?

Considering everything that I have in I life, what am I most grateful for? What about _____ makes me feel grateful?

In what areas do I feel most confident? What makes me feel so confident in that situation?

In what situations do I find myself the most patient? How do I approach those situations to help me to feel patient? Who in my life means the most to me? What makes them so special?

In what types of situations do I feel most relaxed? What about those situations do I find relaxing?

Who in my life loves me? How does that make me feel to be loved like that?

Double Bind

The Double Bind, also known as Alternative Choice, gives the illusion of choice when either response guides you in the same direction. If Kevin asks one of his Professional Mixed Martial Arts fighters, "Do you think you can take this guy?" they basically have three possible responses: Yes, No, or I don't know. If Kevin uses the Double Bind, then it eliminates two of those possible choices: No, and I don't know. Examples of such questions would be:

Do you think you will take him out with striking or submission? Do you think you will finish him in the first round or after that?

For them to answer, they have to *act as if the presupposition were true*, that they indeed would take out their opponent.

Here are some other examples:

- Do you think you will achieve your goal this month or next?
- Do you think you will figure this out yourself or will you work with others?

Milton Erickson, M.D., a psychiatrist, psychotherapist and hypnotherapist, is regarded by many as responsible for legitimizing hypnotherapy for use in psychotherapeutic, medical and dental practices. Erickson was a master of using double binds. In pain control situations, he might make a Double Bind statement such as, "I don't know whether you will begin to feel better today or tomorrow, I really don't know which it will be, today or tomorrow, and you might find yourself being intensely curious about which it will be." Or he might say something to the effect of; "I don't think it would make sense for all of your pain to disappear right away; I think that would be asking too much. I think it would be more appropriate for some of it to disappear, but to have some of it to remain for about three weeks." Please note these are not direct quotes of Dr. Erickson's. Rather, we are trying to give you further examples of the power of double binds.

Winning Mind Set™ Double Bind Exercise

Choose a challenge you have been trying to overcome or resolve and be possibility oriented in your solution using a double blind. Come up with three double binds that you might use:

(1)

(2)

(3)

Possibility Thinking Questions

Some men see things as they are, and say, "Why?"
I dream of things that never were, and say, "Why not?"

- GEORGE BERNARD SHAW

Possibility Thinking Questions help to put us in states where we move beyond any obstacles. Similar in their objective to the Double Bind, these questions help us act as if what we want is possible. They help us delete all the reasons we may not be able to do something, and focus on what we would do *if it were possible*. These are great "antidote" questions to the "I can't / I could never / We'll never / There's no way / I'll never be able to" disease.

- If there were one thing that I needed to concentrate on to take my performance to the next level, what would it be?
- If I did know, what would the answer be?
- If I were able to win, how do I think I would do it?
- If it were possible to do it that quickly, what would I need to focus on?
- If I were able to do this, what would I have to think about? How would I hold myself? (You can bring in the *Physiology of Success* technique).
- If it were possible to do this, how would that feel?
- If there were a way to do this, what would it be?
- In order to achieve this, who would I have to Become?
- If I could pull it off, what would I do first?

Winning Mind Set™ *Possibility Thinking Exercise*

Answer the following possibility thinking questions

1. If there were one thing that I needed to concentrate on to take my performance to the next level, what would it be?

2. Unsure? Ask yourself: If I did know, what would the answer be?

3. If I were able to win or succeed, how do I think I would do it?

4. If it were possible to do it quickly, what would I need to focus on?

5. If I were able to do this, what would I have to think about? How would I hold myself? (You can bring in the Physiology of Success technique).

6. If it were possible to do this, how would that make me feel?

7. If there were a way to do this, what would it be?

8. In order to achieve this, who would I have to Become?

9. If I could pull it off, what would I do first? What initial action step would be most beneficial?

10. In order to succeed, what do I have to say to myself? What self-talk would I use consistently to support my success?

Problem Solving Questions

We will either find a way, or make one.

- HANNIBAL

Problem Solving Questions are designed to help do two things:

1. **Reframe how you feel about the situation**
2. **Focus on taking action towards improving the situation**

Here are some examples of Problem Solving Questions:

- What's actually a positive outcome of this problem? Often when you look back on a situation that was difficult, do you find that it motivated you or forced you to go in a new direction, and it made you do something that you probably wouldn't have done save for the problem? And later on you are actually glad you had the problem?

- What message does being upset communicate? Often this sense of frustration or disappointment always leads to a breakthrough. So, when do you think this breakthrough will come?

- What's not right yet about this situation? This statement presupposes that things will eventually be right, and it gets you to think about what you want to have happen.

- What am I personally willing to do to make things how I want them to be? Am I willing to be flexible, persistent, ask other people, try a different approach?

- What do I need to stop doing (complaining, worrying, procrastinating)?

- What help might I need to get this issue resolved now?

- Who could help me solve this problem?

- Who has already experienced this or something similar?

- How would someone you hold in high regard as a problem solver in that field or area approach this?

Winning Mind Set™ Problem Solving Exercise

Answer the following problem solving questions in relation to a challenge you may be facing or even one you may have struggled with in the past

What's actually a positive outcome of this problem?

What message does being upset communicate to others and myself?

What's not right yet about this situation?

What am I personally willing to do to make things how I want them to be (be flexible, persistent, ask other people, try a different approach, think outside of the problem)?

What do I need to stop doing (complaining, worrying, procrastinating)?

What help might I need to get this issue resolved now?

Who could help me solve this problem?

Who has already experienced this or something similar?

How would _____ approach this challenge?
What would they do?

Figures of Speech

> *The greatest discovery of my generation is that a human being can alter his life by altering his attitudes of mind.*

> - WILLIAM JAMES,
> HARVARD UNIVERSITY PSYCHOLOGIST

The way we look at the world colors how we feel about it. Often times, we choose to represent our experiences through figures of speech that include metaphors, analogies and similes. Examples include:

"Life is a battle."

"I've reached a dead-end."

"I'm going to run into a buzz saw in there."

"Life is a test."

"I'm running into a brick wall."

"Life is a dance."

"I got beat up in there."

"I'm hanging in there."

"I'm at the end of my rope."

"I'm walking on a cloud."

"I'm higher than a kite."

"Business is a game."

"I'm between a rock and a hard place."

"I'm drowning."

"I'm batting a thousand."

"I struck out."

"I'm at Thanksgiving dinner and sitting at the kiddy table."

"I'm playing in the minor leagues."

"That guy is a bear."

"That guy is solid as a rock."

Pay particular attention to the figures of speech that you use. The reason is that while some of these are empowering, such as

"Life is a dance". Where the implications of this metaphor might be that events are flowing, that there is a rhythm to life, that it is fun, relaxing and enjoyable, others can be quite debilitating. Consider the implications of some of the figures of speech of introduced above:

"Life is a battle." The implication is that there are winners and losers, that people get bloodied, injured and killed, that there is a constant struggle. Do you think that a person who viewed the world in this way would relax very often? Or would he be ever vigilant? Would he classify people as either friends or enemies?

"I've reached a dead-end." How do you feel when you reach a dead-end? Lost, angry, frustrated, like you have wasted your time, like you are unsure of where to go next, confused, maybe even scared?

"I'm going to run into a buzz saw in there." An executive with whom Jim worked would say this right before going into a meeting to review the prior month's results. Can you think of a more disempowering metaphor? What frame of mind do you think this executive had walking into those meetings? What level of stress do you think this person experienced each month?

"Life is a test." What are the possible implications here? Some people love tests, others hate them. One might feel a need to prepare, a sense of pressure due to a constant need to perform.

"I'm running into a brick wall." Wow, that would hurt, huh? Using an analogy like this can be very limiting. In real life, what would happen if you ran into a brick wall? You would get hurt, it wouldn't move, you might feel trapped, as if there were no way out.

"I got beat up in there." Another disempowering metaphor. How would it make you feel if you thought of an experience as one where you got beat up? Would you want to do it again? Would you be stressed out going back? If you had to do it again, might you tend to over-prepare?

"I'm hanging in there." Now *that* isn't something you would look forward to.

"It's Thanksgiving dinner, and I'm sitting at the kiddy table." What are the implications of such an analogy used by an executive after a reorganization? That he isn't valued, isn't important, won't be paid attention to, his thoughts aren't appreciated, he won't be included in decisions, he'll be told what to do and expected to do as he is told.

"I'm playing in the minor leagues." What are the implications of this analogy, used by the same executive after a reorganization? The "scouts" won't even come to watch, no one will "see him play", his career is over, he isn't worth as much, and that he is viewed as having a lesser level of talent.

"I'm in over my head!" This analogy implies I may be ready to drown or that I'm sinking and may not make it out.

The image is that of being totally overwhelmed, covered or buried, being in an inescapable predicament with no hope of survival.

You can quickly realize how a seemingly innocent figure of speech can shape one's perception, and concomitantly affect one's emotions. To change the negative metaphors, you can use a technique known as a ***pattern interrupt*** which you will learn more about in the section on **Habits**. This pattern interrupt literally short-circuits a line of reasoning or thinking and creates an emotional opening. It is similar to weakening the legs (references) on the table (beliefs). Once you interrupt your pattern, you find it difficult to feel the same level of emotional intensity about the situation. Once the level of emotion is altered, then you can think about your situation in a more rational manner.

See what we mean below:

"Life is a battle."
>> Which side are you on?
>> Are you a good guy or a bad guy?

"I've reached a dead-end."
>> Better get out your map.

It's time to put it in reverse.

"I'm going to run into a buzz saw in there."

How big is the saw?

Better wear your safety glasses.

"Life is a test."

Do you have your number two pencil?

"I'm running into a brick wall."

What color are the bricks? Are they red, or those tan ones?

"I got beat up in there."

How many rounds did you last? Did you get any good shots in?

Nice gloves. Are they ten or twelve ounce?

"I'm hanging in there."

What happens if you let go?

Wow, you must have a really strong grip by now.

"I'm at the end of my rope."

Does it have a noose?

Is it nylon or cotton?

"I'm between a rock and a hard place."

Is it moldy and slimy?

Are there any grubs or snails there?

"I'm drowning."

Stand up, you're in the shallow end.

"I struck out."

Your average is still good, though.

Maybe so, but you look so cute in your uniform.

"I'm at Thanksgiving dinner and sitting at the kiddy table."

Good, now you can get away with stuff.

"I'm playing in the minor leagues."

Popcorn! Peanuts! Get your ice-cold beer, here!

"That guy is a bear."

What kind, a teddy bear? Grizzly? Polar bear? Koala, Brown, Black, Panda? Can he ride a bicycle? Does he catch fish?

Well, if he is, he has to hibernate some time.

"That guy is solid as a rock."

You sure he isn't a fossil?

Time to get out your hammer and chisel, then.

In a sometimes humorous, sometimes bizarre way, you can interrupt your pattern of thinking and feeling, so that you begin to see things in a more empowering manner.

All perception of truth is the detection of an analogy.

- HENRY DAVID THOREAU

Winning Mind Set™ Reframe Exercise

Come up with three limiting or disempowering figures of speech you may use frequently. Then come up with a pattern interrupt to change the meaning you have attached to each one.

1

2

3

Words

The loudest voice we hear is our own.

- KEITH HARRELL

Jim's yoga and meditation teacher, Gurucharan Singh Khalsa, once asked him which muscle in the body was the strongest. Jim answered that it had to be the muscles in the back or legs. Gurucharan shook his head, "The tongue," he replied. "One word from your tongue can cut down a person immediately, it can destroy them. Or it can lift them up. Don't speak carelessly." It was good advice.

Just as what we say to others can have a major effect on them, the words we use can also have a major effect on us. Consider this. Let's say that you had something bad happen to you, and you use a certain phrase that embraces and utilizes the full extent of the rich and robust English language, such as "This sucks". Okay, so you get upset, and use the phrase "This sucks". You have another negative thing happen to you, and instead of utilizing the full palette of possible expressions in your vocabulary, you generalize your feeling by painting it with the same brush and exclaim, "This sucks". More and more you get into the habit of using that phrase as a reaction to an entire series of negative events.

Over time, don't you think you would begin to associate negative feelings to the word itself? Don't you think that the simple use of that word alone would begin to conjure up a whole history of off-putting experiences and feelings, and in fact intensify your feelings about your present situation? You better believe it would. What would happen if you used another word, one for which you did not have a history of paired emotional linkages, such as the word "distasteful"? Or, a word that has no association for you whatsoever, like "pooky." Can you imagine how you would feel if the next time something bad happened, instead of shouting, "This sucks", you said, "How distasteful"? or "That's pooky" How can anyone get upset using such a word? There's the point.

Take notice of your habitual use of words. The word itself is not as important as the associated states it conjures up. Now remember, we tend to combine a word with voice qualities and physiology to create the entire communication, even with ourselves, that is why in the three techniques above we looked at all of those elements combined. Yet, there remains some value in looking at the use of words in and of themselves and how we associate feelings to them.

We'll share with you three methods you can use to manage your emotions through the use of words:

1. **Get Specific**
2. **Modify**
3. **Substitute and Expand**

Get Specific

Our conscious minds tend to delete, distort and generalize. Sometimes we generalize in order to function in everyday society. We generalize that doors open a certain way, and that allows us to get in and out of places. We generalize that floors will support us when we walk across them, and that prevents us from testing the stability of them with each and every footstep. And we generalize that hot water comes out of the left faucet, and cold on the right, and so we by and large get the temperature of water that we desire.

At times, however, these generalizations get in the way, as you saw in Categorical Beliefs – "All Martians are purple..." and can lead to prejudices and stereotypes. Generalization can also intensify emotions because they make us focus on only a portion of our experiences, instead of the full range. We looked at this briefly in the chapter on **B**eliefs. For example, if an individual said to you, "Nobody can help me with this", that use of language would intensify a feeling of despair, frustration, and hopelessness. Similarly, the use of the word "everybody" in the phrase "Everybody else is in shape there except for me," does the same thing.

Become particularly sensitized to generalizations such as these, and question to check for accuracy, much like questioning a reference for a certain belief:

- All……. All? Who specifically?
- Every…. Every? In which situations specifically?
- Never… Never? Were there any times you did get it right?
- Always….Always? Were there any times that they did not mess up?
- No one….No one? Was there ever a time there was someone?
- Nobody…..Nobody? Was there ever a time there was somebody?
- Everyone…..Everyone? Who specifically?
- It has to be…..It has to be? Why? What would happen if it wasn't?
- Total…..Total? There isn't any aspect that isn't like that?
- Complete…..Complete? 100%, all the way through?

This technique does two things. First, it helps you change from a generality to a specific. That alone tends to reduce the emotional content associated with the situations. Second, it helps you focus on the situation in a different way. By helping to change focus, you help to alter your emotion.

Modify

Modifiers are useful in increasing or decreasing the intensity of an emotion. By utilizing these suggestions, you can help to slightly shift your feelings around a specific situation by using your words differently.

Modifiers that decrease intensity	Modifiers that increase intensity
a bit	extremely
slightly	remarkably
a tad	unbelievably
a little	extraordinarily
moderately	monumentally
fairly	incredibly
mildly	amazingly
somewhat	phenomenally
marginally	outrageously

Substitute and Expand

A quick and easy way to shift an emotion is to substitute overused words with an expanded vocabulary, words for which you most likely don't have much of an emotional attachment, or at least not a disempowering one:

Disempowering or mediocre word / phrase	Substituted / Expanded word / phrase
I'm ...	I'm ...
beat	rest-deprived
whipped	keeping my eyes open
wiped out	not breaking any records
exhausted	bringing up the rear
pissed	wee-weed
angry	peeved
annoyed	on alert
outraged	irked
furious	excited
good	excellent / wonderful

okay	fantastic / raring to go
fine	better than ever / on top of the world
all right	phenomenal / out of this world

Kevin's Winning Mind Set™ Example – What Did You Say?

What we say and how we say it has an amazing power sub-consciously in our determination and perception of the events in our life. I have a friend who said something to me that made me think about just how influential our choice of words and phrases can be toward our perspective, "I have to go to the Gym. I have a really hard time motivating myself. I've been putting it off for two weeks, and I just can't make any more excuses, I have to go."

As I reflected on this statement and the message it projected, I said, "John, maybe you just need to change, I *have* to go to the Gym to I get to go to the Gym?"

John stared at me with disbelief and said, "You're right!" I'm acting like it's a dirty job that I have to do, not something I love." There was no doubt in my mind as to why he had a hard time motivating himself.

Being just as human as the rest of you, we also sometimes find ourselves using words, metaphors or phrases that distort or exaggerate the meaning of something and it absolutely affects the way we view that task or event at that moment. At that moment we will stop and correct ourselves using a positive, empowering twist to our phrase and it always brings a smile to our face.

Let's look at our work time for example. You can always tell when someone hates their job by the way they view time on the job. Do you have four more hours before you get to leave or is your perspective "I only have four more hours left to finish this?" Do you have to do this or do you have the opportunity to do this?

Now, let's focus on competition! Have you ever amplified the meaning of an event with a phrase like, "I got crushed, they killed us or they trashed us!" How about, we were beaten? Now, what do think these statements imply? What sort of images do they conjure up?

What if those were replaced with a de-amplified version, a more realistic description, like, "We didn't play to our potential or we've got some things to work on." These statements portray a different image and a different emotion, don't they?

When we use empowering, solution-oriented statements, they help us see how we can improve our outcome. Negative amplification of events have an opposite effect, because they are problem focused, rather than solution oriented by nature, They have a tendency to make things seem much worse than they were and make it difficult to move to a solution. It's a little hard to recover and shake it off when you're CRUSHED, KILLED, TRASHED or BEATEN.

It's also very hard to ask yourself, what did I learn from this, while licking your emotional wounds, when you've subjected yourself to these very colorful terms.

Winning Mind Set™ Alternative Words & Phrases Exercise

List a few of those words that are disempowering or mediocre that you may tend to use, and then come up with alternative and more empowering words or phrases.

Disempowering word /phrase   Alternative empowering word /phrase

Kevin's Winning Mind Set™ Example – I know I'll make the next one

What you say always matters. I asked one of the best shooters I've met in College Basketball what he thinks about when he misses a shot. His reply was '"Where's the ball? Give me the ball. I missed this shot, I know I'll make the next one." Then when I asked him what he says to himself when he makes a shot. He looked at me quizzically and said, "Give me the ball! I made that shot, I know I'll make the Next!" Interesting that hit or miss, he said almost the same thing each time. Focusing on the solution, rather than the problem. No wonder he was exceptional! He had a Winning Mind Set!

*You've always got to be aware of why you don't win,
otherwise you'll keep losing. Every mistake is a learning
experience and, hopefully,
you won't make the same mistake again.*

- LAYNE BEACHLEY
WORLD SURFING CHAMPION

Using Empowering Substitutes For The Negative Words We Use

How can you use this? Pay attention to the metaphors and analogies you use to describe events for *one week*. Pay particular attention to the figures of speech that you use. The reason is that while some of these are empowering, others can be quite debilitating. Did you get yelled at or was there a difference of opinion? Did you get dumped on or confided in? Was it the worst day or challenging? Are you at the end of your rope or looking for more creative solutions? Are you hanging in there, not too bad, surviving? Or feeling awesome, great, terrific! You get the picture. Now, for that one week, de-amplify the terms that exaggerate the meaning of your negative experiences and amplify the areas that need a boost. Oh, also remember that these are not just the negative words or phrases you say audibly, but the ones you say to yourself using your inner dialog as well.

"No one can make you feel inferior without your consent."

- ELEANOR ROOSEVELT

Remember in life, we don't experience reality. We experience our representation of reality. It is how we Re-present our experiences that determines our outlook on those experiences. Ultimately, it is your outlook that creates your **Winning Mind Set™**!

Emotions
Key Points to Remember

1) There are no bad emotions. Both positive and negative emotions are useful to us. Our emotions can empower us or hinder us. We became aware of and made a list of both our positive and negative emotions we experience regularly.

2) We covered six major techniques that helped us understand and direct our emotions more effectively.

    1) Our physiology
    2) Our breathing
    3) Reframing our interpretations
    4) Asking better questions
    5) Using figures of speech that include metaphors, analogies and similes.
    6) The words that we use to represent our experiences.

3) One of the most dramatic ways we can communicate with ourselves and others is through the applied use of our physiology.

4) One of the quickest ways to change how you feel is to change how

you use your body.

5) How we breathe has an enormous effect on how we feel.

6) Our emotions are dramatically affected by our frame of reference.

7) Remember, we don't experience reality, we experience our representation of reality.

8) The quality of our lives is relative to the quality of our (internal) communication with ourselves and our (external) communication with others.

9) In order to open our minds up to greater possibilities, we need to ask ourselves better questions.

10) We shared with you three methods you can use to manage your emotions through the use of words:

- Get Specific
- Modify
- Substitute and Expand

Results! Why man, I have gotten a lot of results.
I know several thousand things that won't work.

-THOMAS EDISON

Chapter Four

Habits

First we make our habits,
Then our habits make us.

-JOHN DRYDEN

We all have habits. We try to kick and break our bad ones, and form and reinforce those that are good. We have habitual ways of eating. Ever try to eat using your non-dominant hand? We have habitual ways of driving. Ever start driving to work on your day off before you realized you were supposed to be going someplace else? We use words in a habitual way, we make decisions in a habitual way, and we have habits that affect when we eat, go to bed, and get up. We have routine ways of thinking, acting, perceiving, and focusing that we tend not to be aware of at a conscious level. The habitual manners in which we interact and engage with our world have been built up over time, and most are ingrained to such a great extent that our behavior is many respects on autopilot.

A group of construction workers knock off for lunch. One of the guys opens his lunch pail and exclaims, "For cryin' out loud, not peanut butter and jelly again! Every day it's the same thing. I can't stand it."

His buddy says, "Hey, if it bothers you so much, why don't you just ask your wife to make you something else?"

"What do you mean?" he says, "I make my own lunch."

Although this is amusing, the reality is that from time to time we all exhibit habitual behaviors that prevent us from realizing our potential. These habits can be things we do or things that we don't do but should.

"If I do not practice for one day, I know it. If I do not practice the next day, the orchestra knows it. If I do not practice the third day, the whole world knows it."

-IGNACE PADEREWSKI
POLISH PIANIST

A habit is actually just a pattern that has been developed through repetition. Have you ever heard the term "repetition is the mother of skill" or "practice makes perfect?" As a patterned habit is reinforced, it becomes ingrained deeper and deeper into our subconscious. It is the continued repetition of any action or thought that makes that specific action or thought increasingly natural. This is why habits are hard for some people to recognize and difficult for them to alter. There's a saying, "good habits are hard to develop and easy to live with. Bad habits are easy to develop and hard to live with." Yet, doing things in a habitual manner is essential toward our personal development. The more habitual our daily routines and activities become, the less thought and energy we need to use to achieve them freeing up more energy, focus and brainpower to devote to new projects, skills and achievements.

For example; when writing, creative expression can be restrained if you have to concentrate on your typing skills. In another light, by mastering the basic skills of driving a car to the point where it is automatic, you are able to concentrate on conversations with your passengers, study a subject through audio books, or relax and enjoy music. This can all be done without compromising your focus simply because the energy you would use to concentrate on the mechanical actions of driving are automatic from years of practice. In many activities, the more automatic your skills and responses are the more effective you will be.

Let's take a closer look at the structure we use as we learn.

The process of learning a skill is for the most part gradual and repetitious as we pass through four evolving levels of competence.

The first level is known as "unconscious incompetence." This is the primary stage where you have no foundation. You are totally unaware that you lack a certain skill or ability.

The second level is "conscious incompetence." At this level, you lack a particular skill or ability, but know it. You are conscious of your lack of skill. You may even want the desired skill very badly, but are not yet able to move beyond this level.

The third level is "conscious competence." This is the level where you are well aware of you ability and proficient at it.

The final stage is "unconscious competence", a level where you do whatever it is in a state of flow, without the struggle of conscious thought to impede your forward direction. You respond naturally in an excellent fashion. You perform as you are at that moment, a skilled technician without reflection. This is the state that every great musician, athlete, technician, etc. must reach to be exceptional. You just do it!

It would seem that the more aware we are of our undesirable habits, the more likely we are to adjust or change our unproductive habits and cultivate our positive, more desirable habits. Or are we?

Approximately 95 percent of everything you do is determined by your habits, whether they are good or bad. If you keep doing what you've always done, you'll keep getting what you've always gotten. In other words, if you're not getting the results you want, change your approach. Your ultimate goal is to create and practice good habits that will then function on their own to improve your quality of life and direct you toward success.

Pattern Interrupt

One of the most effective methods of changing ones habits is known as a "pattern interrupt". What exactly is a pattern interrupt? Do you remember vinyl record albums? What happens when you put the needle on the record album? It catches in the grooves, and plays the recording, over and over, the same exact way every time, unless... Unless there is a scratch in the record, right? If there is a scratch, what happens? It skips. Once there is a scratch in the record, once the pattern is interrupted, that record can never be played the same way again. It cannot revert to the old habit.

Consider for a moment the common rubber band. Sitting in the drawer, it looks rather unimpressive, but put it on your wrist and you're looking at an ingenious tool for transformation. Choose an undesirable habit you wish to change, and prepare to take action! Every time the bad habit or behavior rears it's ugly head, simply pull back the elastic disciplinary aid and let it SNAP! Once a bright red welt begins to rise on the inside of your wrist, you will begin to see results. At the moment you feel the snap, compound the interruption by saying something like, "that's not me", "I'm more than that" or even just "NO", "erase", "delete". Be sure to use emotion in your statement. This will help to connect with your subconscious.

As your pattern is interrupted, it is essential that you support your action with an alternative, i.e. a positive behavioral change. The old, undesirable habit is now given a replacement: a positive, desirable habit. The rubber band is a simple, yet effective pattern interrupter used by thousands. Not surprisingly, the deeper the pattern, the more interruptions or repetitions of the interruption might be necessary. Also not surprising, the pattern interrupt may be more effective if it is, well….. more intrusive or painful. In order to be successful, it may be necessary to perform the pattern interrupt and a mindful habit replacement a few times until you achieve results. Once you begin to see improvements, try using just the disciplinary self-talk or even visualizing the interruption program in your mind's eye. If you find yourself slipping back into your old behavior, run the program again to reinforce your changes.

Habit is either the best of servants or the worst of masters.

-NATHANIEL EMMONS

Jim's Winning Mind Set™ example
- pattern interrupt

I once worked with an executive who had a bad habit of cutting off other people when he spoke. In meetings, another person would be in the middle of expressing a thought, and he would just start talking as if no one else was speaking. The pleasure he got in the moment was that he got his point out, and that the task at hand was generally accomplished in a much more timely manner. Not many people ever said anything about his habit, since many times he was the most senior person in the room.

The downside of his habit was that although he was well regarded as an intelligent and savvy businessman, and certainly got excellent financial results, he was not seen as a "people person", and so his upward mobility was questionable. And although he was told this by a number of his superiors over time, his behavior did not change. I asked him if he realized what he was doing, and he said that he did, but he felt that in meetings he wanted to get to the point and didn't want to waste time talking. As you might guess he communicated primarily in the visual mode. He knew how other people reacted, and also understood that he needed to develop better communication skills in order to advance in the company, but he said that he just couldn't help it. He could always **see** what the other person was getting at and wanted to get there more quickly. He said that he really did want to curb his habit, but that he just couldn't stop it. It was one thing to talk about it, but in the moment, he would invariably revert to the old interrupting behavior.

In order to coach him, I could have utilized a number of techniques, such as asking him his beliefs about time and relationships, about his understanding of the balance between tasks and maintenance in teams, about the positive and negative impact of his behavior, and why he thought he acted that way. I could have also elicited his values, and gotten him to see how his behavior was or was not in line with his professed value system. I also could have worked with him on his emotional reaction of impatience through a variety of means.

What I did, though, is utilize the technique known as a **Pattern Interrupt** to break his habit of interrupting others.

We worked out a pattern interrupt. Whenever we were in a meeting together, and we often were, and he started to interrupt somebody, I would cough. The first meeting they were in, I had to do it a number of times as he broke into the old pattern. At the second meetings two days later, he started to interrupt someone and then looked over at me. *He* coughed, excused himself for interrupting, and asked the person to continue.

Afterwards, we looked at different ways he could help other people learn to get to the point more quickly in their presentations. Because of his habit of interrupting people, he would always get to the point for them, and thus they never got better at it themselves. Though through his dominance the group arrived at a solution (though maybe not the best solution) more quickly, those around him never got any more efficient in meetings. Once he was able to change his habit through the use of a pattern interrupt, he was able to see that part of his role was to help others learn the same skill instead of totally controlling the situation.

In our opinion, no one has better insight about how to use habits and pattern interrupts than Milton H. Erickson, M.D. If you ever have the opportunity to study his work, we're pretty sure that you will find it extremely worthwhile. Dr. Erickson was renowned for helping people access the resources of their unconscious mind to help them in dealing with and overcoming difficulties they were facing. Trained as a psychiatrist, he is probably best known for his work in hypnotherapy. What many find particularly striking was his amazing ability to understand the patterns of human behavior, and utilize those habits to help his patients overcome their problems.

In times of change, the learners will inherit the earth while the learned will find themselves beautifully equipped to deal with a world that no longer exists.

-ERIC HOFFE

Expand the Habit to Break It

Join the patient.

-MILTON H. ERICKSON, M.D.

Dr. Erickson describes one interaction wherein a woman came to him desiring to lose weight. She was distraught because she could not stop the cycle of gaining and losing, gaining and losing. She would get up to 180 pounds, then go down to 130. After a while she would go back to 180, and return to 130. Over and over, this cycle repeated itself. She was, indeed, at her peak weight of 180 when she sought out his help.

Instead of assisting her in completing yet another cycle of gain and lose, he helped her to interrupt and break the pattern by actually encouraging her habit of overeating. He agreed that he would help her only if she would consent to abide by his orders completely and fully, no matter what. He also told her that she would not like his methods, but that if she agreed, she would have to comply. (Can you see how those instructions in and of themselves begin to break her pattern a bit already? Instead of telling her that he can help her, and it will be easy, he already breaks her pattern by telling her that he can absolutely help her lose the weight and she will hate it.)

Dr. Erickson instructed her not to lose weight, but to gain. He instructed her to eat and eat until she got up to 200 pounds, and only when she got to 200 pounds could she begin to lose weight. Under no circumstances was she to lose the weight until she reached 200 pounds.

Every week she came into his office to get weighed. When she got to 190, she was visibly uncomfortable. She asked him if this was good enough, to which he replied that it wasn't. She came back at 195, and this time she was pleading with him to let her lose the weight (what a different pattern), but he held firm. When she weighed in at 199 she literally begged him to let her lose the weight. He adamantly refused, and told her it was not until she got to 200 pounds that she could begin to lose the weight.

Finally the day came when she weighed in at 200 pounds. She was so thoroughly uncomfortable with her weight that she could not "wait" to lose. When he finally agreed that she could begin to lose the weight, she gratefully and eagerly set about her new task. Dr. Erickson reversed her habitual pattern of lose then gain, to a pattern of gain then lose. What this set up for her was a new habit that any time she would gain, she would automatically want to lose. He also did not fight against her habit of gaining. On the contrary, he not only encouraged it but also *expanded it* by demanding that she gain. He interrupted her pattern of getting "advice" from others about losing weight by requiring her to gain.

Dr. Erickson utilized a similar technique with a six-year-old boy who sucked his thumb. His parents were upset that their son was still sucking his thumb at such an advanced age. They had tried scolding, yelling, and any number of other approaches to get the boy to stop, all to no avail. Finally, they went to see Dr. Erickson. He agreed to work with the boy, but in no uncertain terms instructed the parents that as far as the boy's thumb sucking was concerned, their son was now under his care, and that they were not to say anything about his habit at all.

When he was alone with the boy, Milton Erickson explained that the boy was being selfish. While it was perfectly natural for him to suck his thumb, he was neglecting all of his other fingers. Why he had nine other perfectly good fingers to suck on, and he was only limiting his sucking to just one. He went on and on about how important it was to give all the fingers equal time, and thoroughly encouraged the boy to make sure that every day he sucked on each and every finger for at least five whole minutes. In addition, he said that the boy really ought to get started right away, because for six whole years all of those other fingers had been neglected, so he had a lot of sucking to make up for.

What did Dr. Erickson do? He got him to become conscious of a habit that before was an unconscious act. He also got him to exaggerate and expand his habit, and to extend it to all ten fingers instead of only one. His parents were also told to encourage the boy to suck on all of the fingers as well. Now, this habit was turned into a chore of a minimum of fifty minutes a day of finger sucking. What six year-old is going to want to do that for fifty minutes? That one wasn't, and soon his habit was broken.

So while at times it may be useful to understand the background for why another person may have a certain habit, it may do nothing to change the habit itself to understand its genesis.

It probably comes as no surprise to you the fact that if you put a frog into a pot of boiling hot water, it would immediately jump out because of the drastic change in temperature. But did you know that if you put that same frog into a pot of room temperature water, put it on the stove, and turn on the heat, that the frog will literally boil to death? It's true. Being cold-blooded, the frog will adapt to the gradual change in temperature, it will become accustomed to it, and not notice that it is in an environment that is literally killing it. It is the frog's acceptance of the slow and subtle shift that leads to its doom.

Habits can be the same way. Sometimes we get into bad habits that initially don't seem to be overly negative. Rather, they appear to be just a slight shift in what we had been doing, not noticeable, really. Perhaps it is a few errors in judgment, repeated every day, that can over time land us in hot water!

Utilizing the twin techniques of Pattern Interrupts and Encouragement can help those with whom you work wipe out those debilitating habits.

Jim's Winning Mind Set™ example
- It's hard to quit smoking

In one of my seminars a few years back, we were discussing habits and how to break bad ones, when one of the participants asked a question. "Can you help me quit smoking? I've smoked for over twenty years, and I have never been able to quit for more than a day or two."

Nothing like putting me on the spot. I invited him up front, and asked him to take a seat on the stool next to him. "So you want to stop smoking, huh?" I asked.

"Absolutely," he answered quickly, nodding his head as if to say it would be a good idea as long as he didn't have to do anything differently.

"Absolutely, okay. So, why now? Why after twenty years?" I asked.

"Well, I know it's bad for me," Doug began. I heard a *should* coming, "and I really should quit."

"You really should quit," I repeated. "Meaning?"

"The health reasons."

"The health reasons that you've known about for years, yet you still haven't quit smoking, so …"

"It's hard."

"It is hard to quit smoking, isn't it?" I asked.

"Yeah, it is," he said nodding his head.

"So what's most important to you in your life?" I asked, switching topics.

"My kids," Doug immediately responded.

"Your kids? That's great. What about your kids?"

"That I'm a good role model." Doug's voice changed slightly; it became lower in pitch, and he spoke more slowly. I could tell he was connecting with his feelings very strongly now, whereas before he wasn't.

"That you are a good role model, that's great." I paused. "So tell me, do you want your kids to smoke?"

"No," he said, almost shouting.

"No? Why not? You do it." I insisted.

"I would feel …I just wouldn't. It's a terrible habit, and I would feel like I failed as a father if they smoked."

"You would feel like you failed as a father if they smoked," I parroted back. He nodded. "So tell me, which do you think your kids pay more attention to, what you do or what you say?"

"What I do, definitely."

"I see. So even though you tell them not to smoke, what do you think will happen if you don't stop smoking?"

"They'll probably smoke."

"Probably will smoke, or they will smoke?" I asked.

Doug was motionless with his shoulders slumped. "They will smoke." His voice was barely audible.

"How would that feel, to have your kids smoke? To have them hooked on this nasty habit all because you were not able to quit smoking?" "What kind of role model would you be to them?" I slumped in my stool as well.

"Terrible I know, I …" His voice trailed off.

"How many kids do you have?" Jim asked.

"Two, a boy and a girl."

"And how old is the oldest?" I inquired.

"Tommy is nine, almost ten."

"Almost ten. And how old were you when you started to smoke?"

"Thirteen," he answered.

"So if you don't quit smoking, and didn't have the experience of having no desire to smoke anymore, it will be three years or maybe even less – you know how kids grow up faster these days – until Tommy, is it? Is that his name?"

"Yes, Tommy."

"So three years or less until Tommy begins to smoke, is that right?" I asked. Doug just sat there. He didn't answer. "Is this something you want?"

"No," Doug replied, "I don't."

"Are you willing to change now? To quit smoking and even be free of the desire to smoke?"

"Yes."

"I wonder what would happen if each time you felt like picking up a cigarette, you didn't automatically think about pleasure like you used to in the past, but that you thought about Tommy. That each cigarette, those cigarettes that used to feel so good in your fingers, that you found relaxing in the past, now became a reminder of the positive role model you are now. What do you think your kids will learn from you quitting smoking after over twenty years?" I smiled and sat up just a bit.

Doug smiled slightly. "Um, I think they would learn that they could do whatever they set their minds to." His voice brightened a bit as he sat up.

"They would learn that they could do whatever they set their minds to. What a great lesson for them to be able to learn, and for you to be able to teach them and model for them. After all, they would know that it was hard for you after twenty years to give up smoking, and they would also know that you did it. So they will always have that memory of you quitting and teaching them that you can do anything you put your mind to. How would that feel to you, to know you had that much positive impact?" I said purposefully.

Doug smiled fully now. "It would feel great."

"It does feel great knowing that you have that much positive impact on your children, doesn't it?" I said. Doug nodded his head. "So how do you feel about smoking now?"

Doug grimaced. "Not worth it."

"Not worth it, because?"

"Because I won't be a bad role model to my kids."

"No, you won't. Instead you will be and are a positive role model for your kids, aren't you? And you will continue to be."

"Absolutely" Doug said.

I reached over and shook his hand. His grip was firm, as he looked straight into my eyes. "Congratulations." That was in 1991. Doug has not smoked since.

Winning Mind Set™ Habit Awareness Exercise

Take a moment to think about various positive or desired habit patterns you use to make your life easier or better. List them below.

Great! Now take a moment to think about various negative or undesirable habit patterns you no longer want in your life. List them below. This can sometimes be very challenging because it is hard for us to identify our negative habits. Many of these types of habits are so ingrained that we often don't even realize we are doing them.

Now pick the habit that you like the very least and use the pattern interrupt to change the negative habit to one more desired. Be sure to continue the pattern interrupt until you become conscious of when you are about to perform the negative habit and no longer need the pattern interrupt to aid you. If you find yourself falling back into your negative habit, run the program again. Sometimes just running the program in your head visually over and over will be very effective. In this case you see yourself performing the unproductive habit and then run the interruption program in your head numerous times. We've had great results with this technique.

Performing Edge Visualization is a habit worth pursuing

Visualizing your success is a simple, yet powerful method of predicting your future. Everybody visualizes, just as everybody talks to himself or herself. The empowering difference is when you control what you say to yourself and visualize yourself accomplishing cognitively and consciously you direct yourself mindfully in the direction that will most benefit you. Meaningful achievements begin with a positive vision that we believe in, and commit to with passion. When you learn how to step into that vision, you begin applying all your knowledge, power, and your persistence to turn that vision into reality. When you visualize, visualize your success with as many of your senses, called modalities, as possible. This not only intensifies your clarity, but it also drives the vision deeper into your sub-conscious. Did you know that your sub-conscious cannot distinguish between a visualized event and an experienced event?

The success of your outcome when using visualization will be affected by and relative to these four qualities.

1) **Your Emotional Content-** How well you connect emotionally with your visual imagery.

2) **Your Clarity-** The crystal clear picture you generate in your Mind's Eye while visualizing.

3) **Your Consistency-** How often you saturate your mind with the visual images of what you want.

4) **Your Duration-** The length of time you use visual imagery to focus yourself on your outcome.

Utilizing Visualization To Improve Your Success Ratio

When working with basketball players using the Winning Mind Set™ program, they have improved their shooting remarkably by using this visualization strategy. If you practice for one hour a day and visualize for one hour, you have in effect, completed two hours of shooting. Now here's the question. When you shoot, do you ever miss? Even the best player in the world would have to answer honestly with, "Of course I do." But, how about when you shoot in your mind? 97% of all the athletes we've queried say they always succeed in their imagined visions. So, by shooting baskets (or anything you want to dramatically improve in) in your "mind's eye" for the same period of time, you not only doubled your shooting time, but you just improved your shooting ratio.

Winning Mind Set™ Visualization Exercise #1

Choose a skill you want to improve and become aware of the action and all of the qualities. Later, visualize the action in complete detail. Use your imagination to see the action in as much color and depth as possible. Tune in to as many sounds connected to the event as you can.

Next, imagine as many different physical or tactile feelings associated to the action skill as possible. If there are any smells associated to the event add them to your mental program as you're visualizing your action. Lastly, if you can find any tastes that you connect to the action you are working to improve, place them into your vision. See the scene in your mind's eye as often, consistent, and with as much clarity and detail as you are able.

As you visualize the skill you are trying to improve using these different modalities, you will multiply your effectiveness astronomically.

Winning Mind Set™ Visualization Exercise #2

To improve the proficiency of your visualization skills focus on an event, task or challenge you have in the near future. See yourself approaching the task with a calm, self-assuredness and focused on absolute success. Visualize yourself as though you are looking through a camera, with total sharpness and complete clarity. See yourself standing and feel the emotion of that of total success and completion. Visualize the task you are completing in absolute detail, with the colors, textures, sounds and feelings that make this visualization as real as possible.

Now, see yourself completing the task with complete certainty and boldness. It is as if you were meant to do this effortlessly and masterfully. Once you have completed the event in your mind's eye, begin again at the start as you once again approach the task, this time with even more confidence and familiarity.

Run the visual scene through your head from beginning to end five or six times, each time ending with the absolute success you have achieved completing the challenge with clarity and assurance. When you are ready to approach your task, you will have succeeded at it so many times in your head, that subconsciously, you will have already succeeded. Every great speaker, every great athlete and every great performer uses this amazing technique to assure their success time and time again.

Words Also Become Very Habitual

Take notice of your habitual use of words. The word itself is not as important as the associated states it conjures up. We tend to combine a word with voice qualities and physiology to create the entire communication, even with ourselves. Yet, there remains some value in looking at the use of words in and of themselves and how we associate feelings to them. In the last chapter on Emotions we discussed how we can modify our choice of words in order to amplify or de-amplify our feelings.

When people ask how things are going, we will usually respond "Great" or "Awesome". We have had it proven to us that if we respond that way, we feel that way. We also want you to notice the tone of your voice when you respond "Great". Then, notice the way you feel when you respond with an "OK". Is there a difference? Is the tone of your voice different? We would bet it is! Now, imagine if you responded with great! Awesome! Amazing! Or Terrific every time you are asked, "How are you?" Three, four, five times a day. Do you think that this habitual response might trigger a response in the way you actually feel? Absolutely!

Winning Mind Set™ Word Substitution Exercise

For a period of one week respond mindfully to the questions, "How are you?", How's it Going?", "How you doing?", etc. with GREAT! AWESOME! FANTASTIC! TERRIFIC! Or EXCELLENT! Then ask them how they're doing and notice the response. Most people will seem a little confused or thrown off by your response. And how did they respond verbally? What was the tone in their response? Do this for one day and you will notice a difference in the way you feel. Do this for a week and you will never go back to OK, not too bad, I guess I'm hanging in there.

As previously mentioned, your inner communication also has a tremendous effect on your belief of personal capability, your personal drive and ultimately how you perceive the events in your life. We all communicate with ourselves internally thousands of times a day. We also all have control over what we choose that communication approach to be, and in which direction our self-communication will lead us. You become what you think about most of the time and believe what you tell yourself. Remember to use self talk within the context of

Personal, Positive and Present Tense when communicating what you want and refrain from telling yourself what you don't want.

Habits
Key Points to Remember

1) Our habits are so ingrained in us that our behavior is on autopilot, we are usually not even aware of our actions.

2) Good habits are hard to develop and easy to live with. Bad habits are easy to develop, yet hard to live with.

3) If you keep doing what you've always done, you'll keep getting what you've always gotten.

4) Habits are patterns in our behavior. If we are more aware of these patterns, we are more likely to adjust or change our unproductive habits and cultivate our positive habits.

5) How to use pattern interrupts, to change our patterns of behavior.

6) We learned how to create new successful habits to replace our unproductive habits.

> 1) Clearly identifying your bad or unproductive habit.
> 2) Define your new successful habit in detail.
> 3) Create an action plan with 3 or more steps.

7) We identified both positive and negative habits in our own lives and took steps toward removing the undesirable habits, which affect us in a negative way.

8) We worked on improving our empowering habits in the form of visualization, self talk and word usage in our day-to-day life.

We are what we repeatedly do.
Excellence, then, is not an act, but a habit.

-ARISTOTLE

Chapter Five

Associations

Every man's memory is his private literature.
-ALDOUS HUXLEY

You must have had this happen to you dozens of times. You are in a car driving along listening to the radio, in no particular mood, when a song comes on that reminds you of someone you used to date, and instantly you are in a great mood or a lousy mood, depending on who it was. Right?

Now, here's the question. Did you have to think about it to get that feeling? Did you have to motivate yourself? Shout affirmations at the top of your lungs? Or did it just happen, without any effort on your part?

What about this experience? Do you have a certain food or drink that used to be one of your favorites, that one time made you sick, and to this day you will not touch it? Won't go near it? Have you had this experience? Most people have.

Again, did you have to motivate yourself not to have that food or drink again? Did you have to discipline yourself not to eat it? Did you set goals so you wouldn't go near it? Of course not, that's ridiculous. Yet, to this day chances are extremely high that just the thought, sight or smell makes you feel queasy. At the very least, fair to say you won't be loading up on this delicacy any time soon.

So why? Why is it that you can have an attraction to something for years and years, and then in an instant radically change how you feel about it? How is it that you can have a shift that is so strong that it can literally wipe out years of a conditioned psychological and physical attachment in one fell swoop?

The answer has to do with **associations**. Are you familiar with Ivan Pavlov and his experiments with dogs? He was actually studying gastric secretions in dogs. In the process, though, he noticed something that intrigued him. The dogs were fed at specific intervals, accompanied by a ringing of a bell signaling that it was time to eat. He observed that when the dogs were about to be fed, they would salivate in anticipation of eating. He also learned that the dogs linked being fed to the ringing of the bell, and that they would salivate upon hearing the bell by itself, even without the sight or smell of the food. The bell became linked to eating, and caused the dogs to have a physiological reaction. If you have animals, you know that this phenomenon occurs with can openers, opening a cupboard door, or making a certain whistle.

An *association*, then, is a learned or conditioned linkage between a mental and physical response and a stimulus. In the case of Pavlaov's dogs, the mental and physical response is anticipation of being fed, which produces excitement and salivation. An **anchor** is the stimulus that can **trigger** a certain response, the anchor here being the bell.

Some associations are very strong, and some are fairly mild. What are some common examples? Well, we've already mentioned the song that you hear on a radio. That reaction is an association to feelings in your past. You were in a relationship, feeling peak feelings (let's say that they were positive feelings), and you heard that song. Maybe it was even *your* song. So you had the feelings, heard the song, had the feeling, heard the song, had the feeling, heard the song. Pretty soon, just like Pavlov's dogs, you created an **auditory** association between those feelings and that song. Make sense?

Associations transport us back through time and space in an instant.

Or maybe you hear a song and it puts you into a sad state. Perhaps it reminds you of a time in your life when you were going through a tough time, perhaps you lost someone close to you, and hearing that song brings you back to that time and the associated feelings.

Auditory anchors aren't the only types. The aroma of homemade chocolate chip cookies, or mom's apple pie certainly can evoke powerful memories. The scent of after-shave, perfume or cologne can conjure up strong recollections, too. All of these are examples of *olfactory* associations or *gustatory* if you eat the pie and cookies!

Visual anchors are very powerful as well. That is one reason why many advertisements utilize sex appeal. You see a picture of a sensual model, and get anchored into a state of ... well, whatever state you get anchored into. Positive, no doubt. So you feel the feeling, see the product, feel the feeling, see the product. Pretty soon you link feelings of sex appeal to products like alcohol, cars, clothing, gum and breath mints. You are certainly familiar with this concept from advertising.

What about people? Don't you have reactions/associations to people? Of course. At the office we have a phone with caller ID display. When certain names flash up, we feel a bit of excitement and anticipation about speaking with that person. With others, well, there's always voice mail to pick those up. You are an anchor. What are peoples' associations to you?

What about places? Have you ever taken a dog to the vet for the very first time? It's like, "Oh, happy dog, going for a ride, dum-de-dum, oh let me wag my tail." What about trip number two? Still happy? No way. You bring out your pet cage, or near the vet, and all of a sudden your dog doesn't want anything to do with the place. You could have a little terrier that suddenly feels like it weighs a hundred pounds.

At work, an employee might get reprimanded in the boss's office; they are feeling strong negative feelings, and are in that place. Very quickly they link the negative feelings of intimidation, frustration, anger, or embarrassment, not only to the boss, but also to the room itself. In the same vein, pediatric nurses are told to try and avoid giving shots or medicine to children in their beds so that the kids don't develop a negative association to staying there.

Here are some other examples. An adult student, a woman in her late thirties, was finishing up a bachelor's degree in finance. She was diligent in her studies, and was making excellent grades. In fact, she had a 4.0 average going into her last semester of school. In her third accounting course, though, she was receiving failing grades. She had gotten A's in the previous two, and couldn't understand what the problem was. She said it wasn't the course content. Rather, for some reason she just could not pay attention in class, and had a feeling of anxiety around the professor.

Come to find out, the professor smoked a certain type of pipe tobacco. This woman was sexually abused when she was seven years old by her uncle, who also smoked that type of tobacco. In her unconscious mind, she had linked the odor of that tobacco to understandably negative emotions such as fear, confusion, and humiliation. Though consciously she was not aware of the linkage, her unconscious mind reacted strongly to the trigger of the tobacco, and brought up debilitating emotions from years ago. Luckily she sought help and remedied the situation.

Let us share one more example of how powerful associations can be. Unfortunately this is another example of abuse. In 1993 Jim attended a seminar that dealt with defining and fulfilling your destiny, a program put on by Anthony Robbins called *Your Date with Destiny* ™. During the course of the program, Tony called a number of people onstage to demonstrate a certain concept. One of the participants was a beautiful and vivacious young woman in her early twenties. With an attractive figure and an outgoing personality, she seemed to be enjoying life.

Somewhere during the exercise, she got a hold of the microphone and told a story. She had been sexually abused by a series of disturbed men: her father, her uncle, her brother, and then later on in a number of relationships. On the one hand she wanted the closeness, fun and intimacy a loving, healthy relationship could provide for her. On the other hand, she had an association that being beautiful meant being a target for abuse. It may sound odd, but it is much more common than one might think. In any event, she thought that if she made herself unattractive, that she wouldn't be abused any more by anyone, and so to make sure she wasn't attractive, she pulled all her hair out, strand by strand, since she was a teenager.

Can you imagine how painful that must have been? Yet, to her, the associated pain of potential abuse was more real to her than the current pain of pulling out her hair. Virtually everyone in the audience was in tears listening to her story.

She continued to speak, saying that two weeks prior she had attended an *Unlimited Power* ™ seminar put on by one of my Anthony Robbins & Associates colleagues, "and that was the first time in over thirteen years that I haven't pulled out my hair," she said. With that, she pulled off a red wig to reveal two weeks of stubble on her beautiful head. The room burst into applause.

We share these two stories with you to illustrate just how powerful associations can be. We all have countless associations that we are unaware of consciously; most of them are quite useful. They serve to protect us, save us time, and give us access to powerful and delightful feelings.

Sometimes, however, as in the examples above, associations can be debilitating. A phobia is an extreme form of an association, with an anchor such as an elevator triggering feelings of anxiety and panic.

Winning Mind Set™ Exercise - Finding And Identifying Our Anchors

A very powerful tool for self-improvement and development of our Winning Mind Set™ is to establish and fortify positive anchors, and to eradicate negative anchors that hold us back. It's fun, and can have very satisfying results. First, let's take a moment to become more aware of some of the anchors you have already established.

What positive anchors do you notice in your world? List at least three in each category below.

What visual anchors do you notice and what are the positive or empowering states (emotions) associated with those individual anchors?

What auditory anchors do you notice and what are the positive states you've associated with those individual anchors?

What kinesthetic anchors do you notice and what are the positive states you've associated with those individual anchors?

What olfactory (aroma) anchors do you notice and what are the positive states you've associated with those individual anchors?

What gustatory (taste) anchors do you notice and what are the positive states you've come to associate with those individual anchors?

What negative anchors do you notice in your world? List at least three in each category below.

What visual anchors do you notice and what are the negative or disempowering states (emotions) associated with those individual anchors?

What auditory anchors do you notice and what are the negative states you've associated with those individual anchors?

What kinesthetic anchors do you notice and what are the negative states you've associated with those individual anchors?

What olfactory (aroma) anchors do you notice and what are the negative states you've associated with those individual anchors?

What gustatory (taste) anchors do you notice and what are the negative states you've come to associate with those individual anchors?

Which negative associations you would like to change?

Establishing and Fortifying Positive Anchors

First, let's show you how to establish anchors for yourself. Both of us use anchors to adjust or intensify our emotional state, depending on how we want to perform. We have anchors to increase energy, improve focus, and relax or calm ourselves.

STEP ONE   Determine the state
Determine the state you want to be in. Be very clear and specific about the state. Use positive, personal and present tense orientation when telling yourself what you want. (i.e. "I feel confident, powerful, and

unstoppable, yet relaxed and alert").

STEP TWO   Determine the anchor

Next, determine the anchor that you want to use. In creating anchors, first utilize something you already do when in the chosen emotional state, if possible. Be sure the anchor is unique and includes the kinesthetic action, a personal, positive, present tense verbal statement or key word, and a visualized mental picture of you in that state performing the action while in a peak emotional state.

STEP THREE   Replicate the state as closely as you can

Once you know the state you want to be in, get back into that state. Utilize the modalities (five senses) and sub modalities in as much detail as possible in the form of a success history search and visualization so that you relive the experience as intensely, completely and vividly as possible.

STEP FOUR Set the anchor at the moment of peak feeling

Once you are that peak state, fire off the anchor exactly as it should be.

STEP FIVE   Repeat the process

Now repeat the recipe for anchor at least ten times. This sets the anchor.

STEP SIX   Interrupt your pattern

Stand up, walk around, get a drink, anything to interrupt your previous pattern while anchoring.

STEP SEVEN   Test your new anchor

Last, test your anchor. Fire your prescribed anchor and note your emotional state. You should feel a noticeable difference in the way you feel! If not, repeat the process. If you feel your anchor is losing strength at any point in the future, reinforce the anchor by repeating this process.

If you can dream it, you can do it.

-WALT DISNEY

Jim's Winning Mind Set™ example - On the Mat

"It's all up here," Tim's father told me, pointing to his head. "He has the skills and the conditioning, but he's got to get it together mentally." Tim, a standout second-year varsity wrestler as a ninth-grader, was wrestling in a very competitive weight class in a very competitive tournament, one that drew teams from across the state. Tim had just dropped two matches in a row. In both he had gotten pinned in the first period. Tim had no business being pinned by either opponent, much less in the first two minutes. In fact, he had the talent to beat one if not both guys, but he had appeared flat and lifeless on the mat, almost as if he were only going through the motions. It was a marked contrast to his usual aggressive style.

"I need some mental help," Tim said after his second loss. We chatted for a while, and I invited him to come over to talk before his next match if he was interested. A few days later he called and we set up some time.

"So, what would you like to accomplish today?" I asked as I invited him to take a seat on the couch.

"I don't know."

"You don't know," I repeated, "but you'd like to know, and in fact I bet there is a part of you that already knows."

He nodded his head slowly and crossed his arms in front of his chest.

"In fact, I'm really excited about working with you, and you ought to be excited as well. You ought to be really excited because you possess a very powerful capability, and that powerful capability is the power of your mind. You told me that the reason you lost those two matches last week was purely mental, right?"

"Yeah. I always lose two in a row."

"Oh, so in the past you have always lost two in a row." Tim grinned. "Well, if your mind is so strong that it can influence you to wrestle that way, and you are convinced that your mind is that strong and it was all due to your mind..."

"Yeah."

"Then that same mind can be used in other ways, more positive ways, since your mind is so strong. And you ought to find that very, very exciting as you begin to wonder about how you can begin to use your strong mind in other ways to support you. So why don't you begin this shift now by telling me what is going on."

"I feel so much pressure, like everybody is watching me. I've been on the team since seventh grade, so people expect a lot from me." Indeed, he had wrestled extremely well on the junior varsity team as a seventh grader, and had done well as an eighth and ninth grader on Varsity in a weight class where many of the competitors were juniors and seniors.

"You feel a lot of pressure, and you'd like to feel more relaxed when you are wrestling."

"Yeah. I feel like I can beat anybody, really. In practice, I wrestle great and I feel so relaxed. I do really well against the best guys on the team."

"You do great in practice and feel relaxed, and in competition, you don't feel relaxed but would like to feel relaxed, so sometimes you wrestle great, and sometimes not. What's the difference? Why don't you feel relaxed all the time?"

"In practice there is no pressure. It doesn't matter."

"There is no pressure, and it doesn't matter in practice, and sometimes you feel it does matter in a match."

"Yes," Tim agreed.

"So tell me about your best match. A time when you felt unstoppable, where you wrestled at your absolute best."

Tim smiled broadly as he told me who it was.

"Okay, so against him, you wrestled your best. Why?"

"I knew he was good, he has a reputation, but I just went out there. I don't know."

"I'd like you to remember that match now, and take as long as you need to recall everything you can about that match. You may find you remember it better with your eyes open or closed. I don't really know whether you will remember more with your eyes open or closed, but either way really experience it and feel what it feels like to be in that match now, wrestling at your best."

Tim closed his eyes.

"Are you there?" I inquired.

Tim nodded his head slowly. "Yeah," he breathed, his voice soft and slow.

"How does it feel to be there? How does your body feel?"

"... warm, ready."

"Warm, ready. Do you feel a tension anywhere?"

"...no."

"No, okay. And do you feel that warm and ready feeling equally in your entire body, or is it different in certain locations?"

"...warm, like a machine."

"Warm like a machine. Oiled and smooth?" I suggested.

"Yeah."

"Okay, and as you are in the match now, what are you noticing?"

"Just him."

"You are noticing just him. Is he in color or black and white?"

"Color."

I took notes on what Tim was saying. "That's right, he is in color, and you are feeling warm and ready, only focusing on your opponent, who is in color. Is he dim, bright or normal?"

"... he is bright, but it is like I'm watching it. Like I'm in it, and he is bright, but everything else is dim."

"Okay, he is bright, but everything around it is dim. Is the action fast-paced, slow motion, or normal paced?"

"... the boring parts are fast-forwarded, sped up, but the good parts are slow motion."

"Okay, so the boring parts are fast-forwarded, sped up, and the good parts are slow motion, feeling warm, like a machine, bright, and in front of you, in color, and dim all around." I waited a few moments. "What are you hearing?"

He shakes his head before saying anything. "Nothing."

"You are hearing nothing. Are you saying anything to yourself?"

"... wrestle smart," he said quietly yet confidently.

"Wrestle smart. Okay. So fast-forward to the end of the match, to the point where your hand is being raised. Where you shake hands, and then the ref raises your hand. What do you do or say?"

He grins, and makes a fist with his raised hand. "Yes!"

"When you feel all those wonderful and powerful and relaxed feelings you grin, make a fist and raise your hand."

"I'm there. I feel everything, oh man," Tim laughed.

"You are there, feeling great, having wrestled your best. Okay, you can put your hand down now."

"I don't want to. It feels great."

"It does feel great, doesn't it? Yes, it does, and you can learn to get that same feeling back at any time, so as you drop your hand you can remember that you can get that feeling back any time you wish as you learn how to do that," I offered.

Tim dropped his hand.

"That's right, and so you learn how to get that feeling back now, let's go back to a different match. And the different match is one of the ones you just wrestled."

Tim's body changed visibly. He slumped against the couch, and dropped his head almost into his chest.

"Can you go back there and remember it?" He nodded his head slowly. "So as you are back there, in that match, what do you feel? Hot, cold, or neutral?"

"Cool."

"Cool, okay. What else?"

"Like a coil, like a spring, ready to burst. Like I want to hit something."

"Like a coil, like a spring ready to burst. Like you want to hit something. Okay, and are you in the picture or watching it?"

"I'm in it, but it's like it's happening to me, like it's not real."

"It's not real, and is it bright or dim?"

"It's normal."

"It's normal, and can you see other things besides your opponent?"

"Yeah, everybody in the stands. I can see the looks on their faces."

"Anyone in particular?"

He shook his head.

"Okay, what do their faces look like?"

"They are disappointed, like I let them down."

"They are disappointed, and you don't want them to be, you don't want to let them down."

"No."

"That is certainly understandable that you would want to do your best. Is the action fast-paced, normal, or slow motion?"

"Normal."

"Normal, and are you saying anything to yourself?"

"...jeez, like I can't believe that this is happening."

"Jeez. Can you hear anything else?"

"Yeah, the crowd yelling."

"Can you make out what they are saying?"

"No."

"No. Okay. This picture isn't as much fun to watch, is it?"

Tim shook his head. "No." He opened his eyes.

"What is the worst movie you ever watched?"

"The worst, I don't know."

"Okay, not the worst, maybe, but one that was pretty bad."

"Dude, Where's My Car?"

"Dude, Where's My Car? Pretty bad, huh?"

"Yeah," he laughed.

"Did you see it in a theater or rent it on video?"

"Rented it."

"I see. Did you watch the entire movie?"

"No, about half."

"Only half. Would you watch it again?"

"No."

"Why not?"

"I didn't like it."

"You didn't like it, and it wouldn't make sense to keep playing a tape over and over that you didn't like, would it?"

He agreed that it wouldn't.

"That's right. So tell me, why is it that you believe you have always lost two matches in a row?"

"I just do it. If I lose one then I'll lose another one right after it. It always happens."

"It has in the past always happened, and a lot of thing always happened in the past that don't happen now, and you can think of a lot of examples of that. Even something like wearing a diaper, that used to happen but doesn't happen now, so what was true before really isn't true for you now, is it? So tell me, what did you used to think about after you lost the first match?"

"I felt the pressure, and thought about how bad I did in the first one."

"You played it over and over in your mind," I said.

"Yeah."

"Dude, Where's My Car? Dude, Where's My Car?" Tim laughed. "Where is it? What would happen if every time you began to replay old tapes that you didn't particularly like, for some unknown reason you remembered 'Dude, Where's My Car?' and began to laugh and relax and feel better for some strange reason. I wonder what that would be like, and you can wonder about that too, even though you know how to do that, even if you think you don't know, because you have had that experience so, so many times. You have had that experience of getting something stuck in your head that reminds you of something funny, and you just laugh, and in fact you can't help but laughing because it strikes you as funny, like playing stupid old tapes."

Tim nodded his head in agreement, and in confusion.

"And now that that is done, let's talk about anchoring. You know what it is even if the word is unfamiliar to you. Do you have a song that as soon as you hear it reminds you of someone you once went out with?" He nodded. "And hearing that song puts you in a great mood or a lousy mood without any conscious thought on your part?"

"Yeah."

"That's right, so you already know what anchors are, and in fact already use them when you win. You make a fist and say, 'Yes!' to yourself. So because your mind is so strong this will work very, very well for you. Let's make that connection even stronger now. What I would like you to do is go back to that first match we spoke about. And as you feel very strongly and completely all those positive feelings, when they get to their peak, I want you to make your fist in the exact same way as you do when the ref raises your hand, and say 'Yes!' in the exact same way. Understand?"

Tim agreed that he did.

"So go back to that match, now, feeling warm, like a machine, where it's bright on you and him, and dim around, and you are saying to yourself, 'wrestle smart'.

As Tim replayed the scene over and over, he squeezed his fist repeatedly. "Man, I'm back there," he said beaming. "This is awesome,

I feel exactly like I did."

"Feeling exactly like you did now, double that feeling. Feel twice as good now, as you make your fist and say, 'Yes!' feeling that completely and strongly." We repeated this process a few more times. "Now, I'd like you to stand up. Shake your body out, and sit back down." Tim complied. "What did you have for lunch today?"

"Soup."

"What kind of soup?"

"Chicken broth. I need to make weight."

"You need to make weight. Okay, so now I want you to make your fist and say "Yes!" just like you did before. Fire off your anchor and see how you feel."

Tim did it. His eyes narrowed, and a cocky grin spread over his face.

"How do you feel?"

"Great. I'm back there."

"That's right, you're back there, and you can go back there feeling relaxed and strong at any time. So what I'd like you to do is every time you feel great, whether it is in practice or in a match where you wrestle your best, or in another situation which evokes those same positive feelings, I want you to fire off that anchor by making a fist and saying "Yes!" Each time reinforce those positive feelings, those relaxed feelings, building them up over time so that they are so strong. Then, when you are warming up, fire it off. When you are walking out onto the mat, fire it off. When you are between periods, fire it off. Then, when you win and feel great, reinforce it again, refresh it. Does this make sense?"

"Yes, thank you."

Tim was set to wrestle in the county tournament the next day. He wrestled extremely well in the competition; he was as good as I had seen him. He lost in the semi-finals to a very experienced and talented wrestler, and then proceeded in the next round to trounce his opponent 16 – 1. So much for the "two in a row" curse.

When I look into the future, it's so bright,
it burns my eyes.

-OPRAH WINFREY

Let's revisit the **On the Mat** example to get an even more thorough understanding of what was accomplished and how. Tim wanted to be confident and relaxed while wrestling, but had a limiting (yet factual at least in the short term) belief about losing two matches in a row. We bet if we went back far enough, there would have been instances in which he had lost one match, and then won the next. That would have given him a different reference upon which to focus. Instead, what Jim did was give him the reference of his feelings involved in winning to focus upon in the form of an anchor.

Tim already had an anchor that he utilized, unaware. Moreover, he didn't use it to help get him into a powerful emotional state. Instead, he reinforced an anchor only *after* experiencing positive feelings of success. Tim had a solid belief about losing two matches in a row because his references were built up over a couple of years. In his case, Jim had to interrupt his pattern (you learned about this in the **H**abits section), and teach him how to use an anchor.

Let's review the dialog Jim had with Tim the wrestler from

Jim's perspective.

"So tell me about your best match. A time when you felt unstoppable, where you wrestled at your absolute best." **(I wanted him to get associated with his powerful feelings.)**

Tim smiled broadly as he told me who it was.

"Okay, so against him, you wrestled your best. Why?"

"I knew he was good, he has a reputation, but I just went out there. I don't know."

"I'd like you to *remember that match now*, **(I use an embedded command or suggestion)** and take as long as you need to recall everything you can about that match. You may find you *remember it better* **(suggestion)** with your *eyes open or closed* **(double bind)**. I don't really know whether *you will remember more with your eyes open or closed* **(repeating the double bind)**, but either way really experience it and feel what it feels like to be in that match now, wrestling at your best."

Tim closed his eyes.

"Are you there?" I inquired.

Tim nodded his head slowly. "Yeah," he breathed, his voice soft and slow.

"How does it feel to be there? How does your body feel?" **(Here I want to help him discover how he represents this powerful experience, and to determine which modalities he uses to represent his feelings. I start with kinesthetic because his breathing was slow, and his voice soft, so I knew that he was in a kinesthetic [feeling] mode.)**

"... warm, ready." **(He started with temperature of his body [kinesthetic internal] as opposed to a temperature he would feel outside of his body [kinesthetic external.])**

"Warm, ready. Do you feel a tension anywhere?" (**I wanted to test another kinesthetic sub modality, pressure.**)

"...no." (**He didn't use it to represent his feeling. Actually, that surprised me.**)

"No, okay. And do you feel that warm and ready feeling equally in your entire body, or is it different in certain locations?"

"...warm, like a machine." (**Again, temperature**).

"Warm like a machine. Oiled and smooth?" I suggested. (**I write these down so that I can remember them, and also compare the representational systems used for positive and negative experiences.**)

"Yeah."

"Okay, and as you *are in the match now*, what are you noticing?"

"Just him." (**He switches to the visual modality.**)

"You are noticing just him. Is he in color or black and white?" (**I test the sub modalities of color.**)

"Color."

I took notes on what Tim was saying. "That's right, he is in color, and you are feeling warm and ready, only focusing on your opponent, who is in color. Is he dim, bright or normal?" (**Additional sub modalities for color.**)

"... he is bright, but it is like I'm watching it. Like I'm in it, and he is bright, but everything else is dim." (**Now he is talking about where he is in relation to the picture, as well as the differences between how he is seeing his opponent versus the background.**)

"Okay, he is bright, but everything around it is dim. Is the action fast-paced, slow motion, or normal paced?" (**I reinforce his responses for him, and now turn to the modality of movement.**)

"... the boring parts are fast-forwarded, sped up, but the good parts are slow motion."

"Okay, so the boring parts are fast-forwarded, sped up, and the good parts are slow motion, feeling warm, like a machine, bright, and in front of you, in color, and dim all around." **(Again, I reinforce what he has told me so that the experience is more real for him.)** I waited a few moments. "What are you hearing?" **(Auditory modality).**

He shakes his head before saying anything. "Nothing." **(Interesting – he is in a certain zone where he is for all intents and purposes deaf [auditory external].)**

"You are hearing nothing. Are you saying anything to yourself?" **(Auditory internal.)**

"... wrestle smart," he said quietly yet confidently.

"Wrestle smart. Okay. So fast-forward to the end of the match, to the point where your hand is being raised. Where you shake hands, and then the ref raises your hand. What do you do or say?" **(In this situation, he is in a powerful, positive state. I was curious to learn if he had an anchor already.)**

He *grins*, and makes a fist with his raised hand. "Yes!" **(He did.)**

"When you feel all those wonderful and powerful and relaxed feelings you grin, make a fist and raise your hand."

"I'm there. I feel everything, oh man," Tim laughed. **(It appeared to be fairly strong.)**

"You are there, feeling great, having wrestled your best. Okay, you can put your hand down now."

"I don't want to. It feels great."

"It does feel great, doesn't it? Yes, it does, and you can learn to get that same feeling back at any time, so as you drop your hand you can remember that you can get that feeling back any time you wish as you learn how to do that," I offered.

Tim dropped his hand.

"That's right, and so you learn how to get that feeling back now, let's go back to a different match. And the different match is one of the ones you just wrestled." Tim's body changed visibly. He slumped against the couch, and dropped his head almost into his chest. **(I took note of his physiology.)**

(Next I had him recap a match that did not end well in his opinion, and had him associate to those negative feelings in detail because I wanted to determine if there was a difference in his representational system.)

"Can you go back there and remember it?" He nodded his head slowly. "So as you are back there, in that match, what do you feel? Hot, cold, or neutral?" **(I started with temperature [kinesthetic internal] because that is what he mentioned first before.)**

"Cool." **(This was different.)**

"Cool, okay. What else?" **(Before he said that he felt warm all over, like a machine.)**

"Like a coil, like a spring ready to burst. Like I want to hit something." **(Here there is marked intensity in the kinesthetic internal sub modality. In the successful match, he said he didn't feel any pressure, but in this scenario, the internal feelings are very strong.)**

"Like a coil, like a spring ready to burst. Like you want to hit something. Okay, and are you in the picture or watching it?"

"I'm in it, but it's like it's happening to me, like it's not real." **(He is out of the picture, detached.)**

"It's not real, and is it bright or dim?"

"It's normal." **(This is different.)**

"It's normal, and can you see other things besides your opponent?"

"Yeah, everybody in the stands. I can see the looks on their faces." **(Before, he and his opponent were bright, and everything else was dim.)**

"Anyone in particular?"

He shook his head.

"Okay, what do their faces look like?"

"They are disappointed, like I let them down." **(This is important, though he can't see anyone's face in particular, he has a sense that he has let others down.)**

"They are disappointed, and you don't want them to be, you don't want to let them down."

"No."

"That is certainly understandable that you would want to do your best. Is the action fast-paced, normal, or slow motion?"

"Normal." **(The speed of the visual modality is different here as well.)**

"Normal, and are you saying anything to yourself?"

"...jeez, like I can't believe that this is happening." **(Markedly different content and quality of his voice.)**

"Jeez. Can you hear anything else?"

"Yeah, the crowd yelling." **(Recall that he was "deaf" before; now he can hear and see everything.)**

"Can you make out what they are saying?"

"No."

"No. Okay. This picture isn't as much fun to watch, is it?"

Tim shook his head. "No." He opened his eyes.

(In the first, positive experience, it was if Tim was deaf and

near-sighted. He was unconsciously choosing to use only certain parts of his brain and body. In the second, negative experience, Tim represented his experience in a much different way. He was hypersensitive to sound and sight, and had a disempowering tension in his body.)

(After Tim recalled his negative experience, and got fully associated to those tense and hesitant feelings, he was even more eager to learn how to use an anchor to trigger those positive feelings he had experienced before. I then spent some time giving him a pattern interrupt to use.)

"And now that that is done, let's talk about anchoring. You know what it is even if the word is unfamiliar to you. Do you have a song that as soon as you hear it reminds you of someone you once went out with?" (**Here I give him an example that I know he will relate to.**) He nodded. "And hearing that song puts you in a great mood or a lousy mood without any conscious thought on your part?"

"Yeah."

"That's right, so you already know what anchors are, and in fact already use them when you win. You make a fist and say, 'Yes!' to yourself. So because *your mind is so strong this will work very, very well for you.* (**I am pointing something out that is true, and I am giving him a suggestion.**) Let's make that connection even stronger now. What I would like you to do is *go back to that first match we spoke about.* (**I have him go back to a specific situation and experience all of those positive feelings.**) And as you *feel very strongly and completely* all those positive feelings, ***when they get to their peak***, I want you to ***make your fist in the exact same way*** as you do when the *ref raises your hand* (**moment of peak positive feelings.**) and *say 'Yes!'* in the ***exact** same way.* (**The way we say things [voice qualities] affects the meaning of communication [38%], even with** ourselves. **So I wanted him to be sure to say the words in the exact same way, same pace, tone, and pitch.)** Understand?"

Tim agreed that he did.

"So go back to that match, *now*, **(suggestion)** feeling warm, like a machine, **(his analogy)** where it's bright **(near-sighted)** on you and him, and dim around **(doesn't focus on that, in effect he can't see it)**, and you are saying to yourself, "wrestle smart" **(no other noises – he is "deaf." I remind him of all the modalities [i.e. kinesthetic, auditory, visual] and sub modalities [temperature, brightness level, volume] by which he represents his positive experience.)**

As Tim replayed the scene over and over, he squeezed his fist repeatedly. "Man, I'm back there," he said beaming. "This is awesome, I feel exactly like I did."

"Feeling exactly like you did, *now*, **(again, a suggestion to go back in time to that experience in the past)** double that feeling. *Feel twice as good now*, **(here I ask him to imagine the feeling as being twice as strong in order to strengthen the anchor)** as you make your fist and say, 'Yes!' *feeling that completely and strongly*." We repeated this process a few more times. "Now, I'd like you to stand up. Shake your body out, **(here I am interrupting his pattern by changing his physiology – I want him to get out of that positive state so we can test it to see how strong the anchor is)** and sit back down." Tim complied. "What did you have for lunch today?" **(I interrupt his pattern by asking him a totally irrelevant question.)**

"Soup."

"What kind of soup?" **(Insuring that he is completely out of the positive state. He's probably thinking, "What is wrong with this guy? Is he nuts?")**

"Chicken broth. I need to make weight."

"You need to make weight. Okay, so now I want you to make

your fist and say, "Yes!" just like you did before. Fire off your anchor and see how you feel." (**I'm asking him to replicate the anchor**).

Tim did it. His eyes narrowed, and a cocky grin spread over his face.

"How do you feel?" (**I question him to determine how strong it is, but I also rely on my own observations – not simply his words [which represent only 7% of communication], but on how he says those words [38% is determined by voice quality], and what his body language [55% of communication is conveyed through body language] is telling me.**)

"Great. I'm back there."

"That's right, you're back there, and you can go back there feeling relaxed and strong at any time. So what I'd like you to do is every time you feel great, whether it is in practice or in a match where you wrestle your best, or in another situation which evokes those same positive feelings, I want you to fire off that anchor by making a fist and saying 'Yes!' Each time reinforce those positive feelings, those relaxed feelings, building them up over time so that they are so strong. Then, when you are warming up, fire it off. When you are walking out onto the mat, fire it off. When you are between periods, fire it off. Then, when you win and feel great, reinforce it again and refresh it. Does this make sense?" (**This step is critical. In order to overcome his limiting feelings of tension, pressure and despair, he needs to have very powerful feelings of success, confidence, and relaxed alertness. By reinforcing his positive anchor over and over, it will become stronger and stronger. He does not have to limit the reinforcement to success in wrestling alone. He could have a powerful feeling from an entirely different experience, yet still anchor those feelings to the making of his fist, and saying, 'Yes!'**)

There is a law in psychology that says if you form a picture in your mind of what you would like to be, and keep that picture there long enough, you will soon become exactly as you have been thinking.

-WILLIAM JAMES

Eliminating Negative Associations or Anchors

As you by now realize, associations are extremely powerful. They break through barriers of time and space. When you hear a song that reminds you of someone you used to date, your thought processes, physical and emotional reactions are remarkably similar to when you first had that experience. Decades can melt away in an instant as you are transported back in time.

Research done in hypnosis by Platnow and Erickson back in the 1930's revealed that adult subjects who were regressed through hypnotism, and who thus believed that they were indeed children who had not yet become adults, consistently performed on intelligence tests as if they were children. Moreover, when tested for emotional and even muscular reflex responses, they performed in a way consistent with that of a child. When adult control groups were asked to "act" as children, they did not come close to approximating the responses of the regressed adults or actual children.

We bring up this research to illustrate the point that we all have the capability to go back in time physically and mentally. Associations have a way of doing that quite powerfully, dramatically and rapidly.

Do you recall the example of the woman and her professor and the pipe? So even if an individual has a certain learned capacity to deal with situations in the present time, chronological age and stage of development, associations have a way of regressing us to a period when we may not have had the same skill set. Did the woman with a 4.0 grade point average engage intelligently and effectively with her situation when she smelled the pipe tobacco? Hardly. She felt confused and scared, and worst of all, she didn't even know why. Do adults, when visiting their parents, have a tendency to fall back into old patterns of behavior when surrounded by the sights, sounds, smells, tastes and people from their childhood? You better believe it.

One of the points that counselors stress in drug, alcohol or behavioral rehabilitation is for former addicts to stay away from their prior peer group associated with the damaging, negative behavior. It has been found over and over that even totally rehabilitated drug addicts and alcoholics will slide right back into their former life when they are placed back in their previous (addictive) enviornment.

How, then, do you deal with a situation where you have an immediate negative or disempowering reaction to a person, place or situation? It's one thing to create a positive association by using an anchor, but how do you overcome a negative one?

The good news is that you can use many of the techniques that you have already learned in order to do that. You can use state-inducing questions, possibility questions, reframing, beliefs, breathing, and expanding the habit. In addition, we'll share with you three more specific approaches you can use.

Changing the Past

You know that a negative association is a way of representing or remembering a situation or experience that is disempowering, right? We tend to focus or process information in a certain way which elicits certain emotional and physical responses. We feel a certain way because we think a certain way through various modes (or modalities). When we change the way we represent our thought processes, we will change how we feel and very often our resultant behavior.

Altering sub modalities quickly changes how we "remember" a situation. In effect, it changes our past because the way we remember our experience is different. Since our memory of the event is different, our emotional reaction to it is different, and so our association is as well. Since our association has changed, our present reaction also changes.

Here's the exercise. Pick an experience that you feel is negative and disempowering. That is, one which, when you think about it, makes you feel sad, angry, helpless, lonely or hurt. Just as Jim did with Tim, go through and list out how you represent this scene in your mind. You can do it yourself, or you can ask a friend to ask you the questions and take notes so that you can concentrate. Go through the list of modalities and sub modalities below.

Representational System: Modalities and Sub Modalities

Visual Modality	Questions to ask
Color / black and white	Is it in color or black and white?
Specific color	Does any one color in particular stand out for you?
Movement	Is it a still-frame, or moving?

Pace of movement	Is it normal paced, sped up, or slow motion?
Continuity	Does the pace vary or is it constant?
Brightness	Is the picture bright, normal, dim, or dark?
Clarity	Is it clear or fuzzy, does it vary depending on the content of the picture?
Distance	Are you far away from, near, or in the picture?
Perspective	Where are you in relation to the picture, above, in, below?
Dimension	Is it in 3-D, or is it two dimensional like a photograph?
Focus	Are some parts of the picture in better focus?
Size	Is the picture life size, bigger or smaller?
Span of vision	Does the picture fill up your vision, or concentrated in one specific area?
Specific visual element	Is there anything else that you see that is important to you?

Auditory Modality	Questions to ask
Content	What specifically do you hear?
Self-talk vs. other sounds	What are you saying to yourself? What sounds do you hear ?
Pace	Are the sounds sped up, normal paced, or in slow motion? Does it vary?

Location	Where are the sounds coming from?
Volume	What about the volume of the sounds, are they quiet, normal, or loud?
Constancy	Are the sounds constant in nature, or do they vary? If so, how?
Inflection	Is there much inflection in the voice, or is it more monotone?
Words	Are there certain words that you hear?
Duration	How long do the sounds last?
Pitch	Are the sounds high, medium or low-pitched?
Pleasantness	Is it pleasant to listen to the sounds, or are they disturbing to listen to?
Others sounds	Are there any other sounds that you are hearing?

Kinesthetic Modality	Questions to ask
Temperature external	Do you feel the outside temperature? Hot, warm, body-temp, cool or cold?
Temperature internal	How do you feel inside: hot, warm, normal, cool, or cold?
Constancy of temperature	Is the temperature the same all over, or does it vary or drop off anywhere?
Pressure external	Do you feel a pressure on you? What does that feel like?
Pressure internal	Do you feel a sense of pressure inside your body? Where? How's it feel?

Constancy of pressure	Does the pressure change or is it constant?
Breathing	Is your breathing full and deep, normal, or shallow and fast?
Rhythm	Does the feeling possess a rhythmic quality to it? If so, what?
Speed	Does the feeling have a certain speed? If so, what is it?
Constancy of speed	Does the speed vary or is it constant?
Loose / tight	Do you feel relaxed and loose / tight & tense in certain parts of your body?
Tactile sensations - smoothness	Does it feel rough or smooth?
Tactile sensations – wet / dry	Does it feel wet or dry?
Shape and size	Does it have a certain shape or size?
Constancy of shape / size	Does the size / shape change, or remain constant?
Weight	Do you feel heavy, normal, or light?
Other feelings / sensations	Are there any other feelings or sensations that you are experiencing?

Not all of these modalities will be of equal importance. You might discover that one or two modalities can instantly impact your state. Once you have the list, go back through or have a friend help you, and change the modality. Like the experience of going to an optometrist where he changes the lenses and asks, "Better or worse?" See which modalities really impact your "experience" of the memory.

Once you do, replay your memory again with the altered modalities. We'll bet that your emotional state will be significantly altered.

Change Your Physiology

Remember from the section on Emotions that one of the quickest ways to alter your emotions is to alter the way you use your body? For this Winning Mind Set™ tool, you will use a powerful physiology to destroy the disempowering association. Here's how to do it.

Get into the most powerful physiology you can muster. Either remember a time you felt powerful, or imagine yourself or a role model that way. When you are feeling great, think about the negative association, but make sure that you don't alter any aspect of your physiology. Be sure to keep breathing the same way, with the same facial expression, and that your eyes keep looking in the same direction. Keep thinking about that image, but make your physiology even stronger. Come one, double the intensity. Even stronger!

Our bet is that one of two things will happen. Either you will have virtually no negative association at all with the image, or that you will have trouble even remembering the image in that powerful state. Give it a try.

Scramble Technique

This one is a lot of fun. Think about a association that you would like to change. One where when you see, hear or think about a person or situation you go to "a bad place." That is, you get angry, sad, lonely, hurt, etc. The goal here is to discover your disempowering *pattern*. Just like Tim had an "I don't want to wrestle this guy" pattern, you have one for your disempowering association. And, just like the sub modality exercise, you need to discover exactly what your pattern is. This is also one that you can do yourself or get the help of a friend.

Let's apply this to an "overwhelmed" pattern:

1. What do you say to yourself when you get the feeling of being overwhelmed? Think of a specific example and go back there now. Even if you only say it to yourself or under your breath, what is it? Say it out loud for this exercise.

2. How do you say it? What kind of tone, pace, inflection, volume? Say it exactly the way you say it to be "overwhelmed."

3. How do you move? Do you make a certain gesture? Do you hold yourself in a certain way? Are you sitting? Slumped? Standing?

4. What feelings do you have? Do you feel a certain pressure anywhere? Tightness? Any feelings of temperature?

Replay your pattern exactly. Once you have it down, go through the following procedure:

STEP ONE

For one minute, list all the benefits of your pattern. Even though you may logically think that your behavior is counterproductive, at least at the level of your subconscious you must have some reason for holding on to this pattern.

STEP TWO

For another minute, explain all the negative effects of having this pattern. How does it make you feel, what does it prevent you from doing, how does it impact your energy level, how does it make your insides feel? Go into as much detail as possible.

STEP THREE

For a final minute, talk about why you want to change this pattern of behavior.

STEP FOUR

Recreate your pattern six different ways.

1. The first time, recreate it exactly as you do normally, but do it

seven times in a row.

2. The second set, run your pattern in super-slow motion six times. That means all your motions, speech and breathing are slowed way down.

3. For the third set, run your pattern seven times backwards. Your words have to be backwards, and your movements. If you have a overwhelm pattern which includes you saying, "How can I possibly get all of this done?" you'll say, "Done this of all get possibly I can how?" Sounds kind of like Yoda!

4. For the fourth set, repeat your pattern eight times like a spoiled little three-year old having a temper tantrum. Really go for it!

5. For the fifth set, repeat this pattern as your favorite celebrity. Do this nine times.

6. Finally, for the last set, repeat your pattern as a proper British butler six times.

You can alter the characters as you see fit; the point is to have you "scramble" your recollection of the pattern. This is a form of pattern interrupt that you learned about in the **Habits** chapter. A lot of people opt out of the Scramble technique because they think it is too weird. It is! It is also very effective for just that very reason. When you try to go back to your original pattern, it is impossible. If you don't laugh, at a minimum you feel neutral, which is generally a notable improvement from what you felt before.

Associations are powerful, both in a positive and negative way. Your ability to unleash your full potential will be in some part determined by how well you harness and direct the power of your associations.

Associations
Key Points To Remember

1) An association is a learned or conditioned link between a mental and physical stimulus of some kind.

2) An anchor is a stimulus that can trigger a certain response; I.E., an anchor is a created association between a specific trigger and a specific state.

3) Anchors are created when a person is fully associated in an intense emotional state.

4) Anchors can be either positive or negative in nature.

5) A phobia is an extreme example of an association with the "fear" acting as a negative anchor for the phobic individual.

6) Anchors can be in the form of a single or combination of five modalities or senses:
    A) Visual Anchors
    B) Auditory Anchors (internal or external)

C) Kinesthetic Anchors (internal or external)

D) Olfactory (smell) Anchors

E) Gustatory (taste) Anchors

7) We learned seven steps to setting and anchor.

A) Determine the specific state you want to be in (anchor).

B) Determine the anchor. Is it something you already do without realizing it? Remember to try to anchor using as many primary modalities as possible for maximum effectiveness.

C) Replicate the state as closely as possible using the primary and sub-modalities in as much detail as possible.

D) Set the anchor at the peak state of full association.

E) Get out of the state by interrupting your pattern.

F) Test your anchor!

G) Reinforce your anchor regularly.

8) We can increase the power of our anchors by using our physiology in an empowering way.

9) We can overcome negative associations or anchors by changing the way we remember events (modalities), changing our physiology, or scrambling our disempowering patterns.

*Winning in any competitive arena,
whether it be sports or business,
first takes winning in your mind.
If you can win in your mind,
you can win anywhere.*

- ERIK CHARLES

Chapter Six

Values

Carefully observe what way your heart draws you and then choose that way with all your strength.

-HASIDIC PROVERB

Jim has a story about a personal experience he had that helps us begin our journey into our next chapter's subject: values.

I remember back in 1982, driving with my sister and her boyfriend to New York City. My wife, then girlfriend at the time, lived there, and I was going to see her, and my sister and her boyfriend were going to visit friends. We were engaged in conversation, and I, having driven the trip a number of times previously, wasn't really paying attention to where I was going. I was supposed to be in the lane for route 95 to the George Washington Bridge, but I was in the lane for route 80 east headed for the Oranges in New Jersey. By the time I realized it, it was too late to change. I was stuck going in the wrong direction. As I was driving, I was heading further and further away from where I really wanted to go.

Amazingly enough, we couldn't turn around for almost twenty miles, and you know how frustrating that can be when you know exactly where you want to go, but are not going that way. Worse, though, is when you are completely lost and have no idea where to go, but you know the road you're on is wrong.

Has that ever happened to you? In a car, most definitely; but what about life? Have there been times when you felt uncertain about your direction, about where you were heading? Have there been times when you had an uneasy feeling about how you were spending your time, and maybe about what you were running after?

A lot of people tend to go from job to job to job, or city to city to city, or relationship to relationship to relationship, seeking something. Many times they get very, very good at knowing what they don't want, but have difficulty pinpointing exactly what they do want.

We'll let you in on a secret. Nobody wants money, material possessions, or even close relationships. Now before you declare me crazy, think about it. Have you ever had a total crush on someone? You thought about that person, and you fantasized about what it would be like to be with that person, and you had this entire vision in your mind about how great it would be to go out with that person ... until you did? And then you were like, "What was I *thinking*?"

Why? You were enamored with the *idea* of that person. You were caught up in what you thought would be the *emotions* you would feel if you were to be with him or her, not the person him or herself.

Values and Avoided States

Have you ever achieved something and thought, "Is this it? Is this all there is?" We all have things that we want – the relationships, the money, the cars, boats, clothes, homes, and so forth – but the reality is that **we want the emotions that we believe those things will give us**. We want the closeness, the love, the trust, the humor, the intimacy and the sharing that a relationship can bring. We want the security, the freedom, the power, and the sense of accomplishment that money can bring, and we want the excitement, the prestige, the status, and the fun we believe certain material goods will afford us.

But haven't we all had the experience where the relationship brought certain degrees of pain, hurt, mistrust, or betrayal? Where having money meant hassles, tension, and pressure? Where having material goods caused us more aggravation than anything else (or at least it may have seemed it at the time)? All these things, the cars, money, relationships, etc., were means to an end. They were ways we thought we could get the emotions that we wanted, emotions we valued. Therefore, what we really wanted were the *values* of love, success, fun, excitement, security, and on and on. **A *value* is an emotional state; *your* values are emotional states that are important to you.**

For example, adventure is a value; it is an emotional state. Adventure may not, however, be one of *your* values in that it is not an emotion that you find particularly appealing to you; it is not an emotional state that you deem important.

We don't want the things – money, cars, and relationships – as much as we desire the *emotional states* we think those things can give us.

Values provide a powerful motivating force for behavior. After all, we all desire to have pleasure in our lives. Yet, it is also useful, indeed vital, to understand what others link pain to. Just as we all link varying degrees of pleasure to values, we link varying degrees of pain to emotional states such as boredom, rejection, loneliness, failure, jealousy, and so on. These emotional states are ones we try to avoid, so we call them *Avoided States*. We link pleasure to values, and pain to avoided states.

Many times, people identify their values and set goals to link up with these desired states, acting as if pleasure is the only driving force in a person's life; anything feared or avoided is almost not to be spoken about. Yet, looking at pleasures is only part of the equation. Unless you are aware of what a person also links pain to, it is difficult to help motivate them.

For example, a person has just gone through a particularly nasty, bitter divorce. A relationship that began with feelings of love, closeness, trust, and fun might have ended in feelings of betrayal, hatred, anger, frustration and sadness. After a time that individual might be interested in pursuing another relationship, but finds that she shies away from commitment. Why? One reason is that for her, psychologically, a relationship (the means) no longer equals pure pleasure. In fact, she may link or associate a relationship to both pleasure and pain. She certainly has enough personal references for both, and probably with the experience of an acrimonious divorce, enough second-hand references about relationships being negative as well from well-intentioned friends and family who also have had negative, painful experiences that they are willing to share ("men are pigs"/ "women will take you for everything you have").

It may be helpful to think of values and avoided states as two sides of a scale. So you have the "means," such as a relationship, in the middle, and "values" and "avoided states" on either side:

Means
Relationship

Values	Avoided States
Love	Pettiness
Trust	Distrust
Closeness	Anger
Togetherness	Alienation
Intimacy	Frustration
Fun	Humiliation

For this example, if we had an individual who wanted to date again, it would be important to determine where they were in this balance. Typically, if someone has a mixed association toward what something means to him or her, you see a behavior we call in psychology "Approach – Avoidance." That is where someone has an initial attraction for something or someone, but then pulls back because a part of them does not want it.

Think about other examples of approach – avoidance. Someone wants a promotion. She values success, feelings of accomplishment, freedom due to a higher income, and making a difference, yet may not want it at the same time. Her avoided states being a belief that she will spend more time at work and less with family, which equates to feeling loss of love, closeness and perceived pressure. Perhaps she feels like she would have to alter relationships with co-workers, and links this to a feeling of superiority, something she else wants to avoid.

A salesperson wants to be successful, but fears rejection; an athlete has a desire to improve, but fears failure; a person wants to make new friends, but fears that he or she won't know what to say, imagining humiliation, nervousness and awkwardness. Get the idea?

Six Steps to Identifying a Value System

There are six steps to utilizing values effectively:

STEP 1	Identify all Values and Avoided States
STEP 2	Put the Values and Avoided States into a Prioritized Hierarchy
STEP 3	Identify any conflicts between or within pain and pleasure states
STEP 4	Identify rules for determining Values and Avoided States
STEP 5	Make changes in rules and hierarchies to align with objectives
STEP 6	Create action plans that are in alignment with Values and Avoided States

STEP 1   Identify all Values and Avoided States

This can seem like a daunting task given that there are roughly **4,000** emotions in the English language. Interestingly, or maybe unfortunately, there are about **1,000** emotions that describe positive states, and around **3,000** that describe negatives states.

Below are a few questions that can help give you some insight into what is or is not important to you.

Winning Mind Set™ Exercise – Identifying Values

What is the best compliment someone could give you? Why?

If you were to appear on a cover of a magazine, which magazine would you want it to be and what would you want the article be about?

How would you spend your time if you had all the money you ever needed?

If your life were ending now, what would you regret not having done?

What are your fondest memories? What about those memories is important to you?

What do you want to have (material good or personal quality) that you don't have now?

What is your fantasy job?

If you had a magic wand that could make you start doing one thing you currently aren't doing, what would it be?

What is most important to you in your life? What about that is important?

What would you do if you knew it was impossible for you to fail?

Which three accomplishments are you most proud of? What about them makes you proud?

What award would you most like to win? Why?

Who do you most admire? What attributes do they possess that you wish you had to a greater extent?

Using Questions to elicit Avoided States:

What would be the worse thing your boss / teacher / coach could write or say on or about your performance assessment / report card / performance?

What events in your memory are the most painful for you? What about them makes them painful?

What things in your life do you say you want, but not take action on? Why not?

What kinds of things tend to frustrate, annoy or irritate you the most? Why is that?

What kinds of behavior in others bother you the most? Why is that?

What do you want to release or eliminate in your life right now? Why is that?

When you are having a "bad day", what kinds of behaviors might you demonstrate that you later regret?

If you had a magic wand that could make you stop doing one thing, what would it be?

You can jot down the answers to these questions to help you focus more directly on your inner feelings. This will also help expound upon any areas that are unclear by asking yourself follow-up clarifying questions such as, "What about that makes me ..." or "What would having _____ give me in terms of a feeling? How would that make me feel?"

"The best and most beautiful things in the world cannot be seen or even touched.
They must be felt with the heart."

-HELEN KELLER

Winning Mind Set™ Exercise –Assessing Values and Avoided States

Create a list of *Values* on one side of a page, and *Avoided States* on the other side. Then review it closely and see if anything is missing. States can always be added, so be careful about taking any off at this point since sometimes we judge ourselves thinking we *shouldn't* feel that way, or we really *should* feel this way. Simply let whatever comes out sit for the time being. There is no right or wrong number of feelings. Just go as long as there seems to be interest and energy, or until the answers begin to become repetitive.

Values	Avoided States

STEP 2 Put the Values and Avoided States into a Prioritized Hierarchy

Once you have a list of values, look it over and put each side in a hierarchy. This will help you understand your overall priorities in life in terms of values, and help identify those negative emotions that you may tend to avoid most. **You can ask questions such as these to elicit a hierarchy in Values:**

1. If you could only have six values, six emotional states in your life, which six would they be? If you could only have five, four, three, two, and one?

2. When you spoke about your most positive memories, this value kept popping up. Would you say that that is one of the most important ones for you?

You can ask questions such as these to elicit a hierarchy in Avoided States:

1. What would you most want to avoid in life?

2. When you spoke about your most negative memories, this emotion kept coming up. Would you say that that is one you would most like to avoid?

3. If you could never again feel six emotions, which six would they be? Which five, four, three, two, and one?

Hierarchy for Values	Hierarchy for Avoided States
1	1
2	2
3	3
4	4
5	5
6	6
7	7
8	8
9	9
10	10

There is no right or wrong number to be in a hierarchy. In general, ten is probably the upper limit that you might work with. There usually are five to eight values that have the most influence over our behavior, and three to five avoided states that most impact us as well.

STEP 3 Identify any conflicts between or within pain and pleasure states

Let's say that you have built the following list:

Hierarchy for Values		Hierarchy for Avoided States	
1	Love	1	Unloved
2	Making a difference	2	Purposelessness
3	Achievement	3	Useless
4	Feeling valued	4	Rejection
5	Trust	5	Mistrust
6	Health	6	
7	Learning	7	

First, notice any conflicts that may exist within your values hierarchy. For example, Jim once worked with a gentleman named Keith who sold insurance. He was one of the top salespeople in his office of about fifty people. Those results were certainly consistent with his values of achievement (you'll see why this may not be an unqualified yes when we get to **Rules**, though). Love was his top value, as it is for many people. He also wanted to lose about 70 pounds. Now, to look at him, you may agree that he had 70 pounds to lose, but you probably wouldn't surmise that health was one of his top values. After all the values that he could possibly pick, to have health as number 6, you'd think he would be healthier.

But here was the situation as he saw it or more accurately felt it. Health really was important to him. In high school and college he was quite an athlete. As he got into the work routine, though, and as he and his wife began to have children, he found himself spending more and more time with his family. No surprise, since love was his highest value.

He would get to a point, however, where he would get disgusted with how he looked and felt. Then he would go join a gym, and work out for about a month, but would invariably quit. Why, because it took too long to get results? No. The reason was, who was he not spending time with while he was at the gym? His family. So what value wasn't being met? Love. Bingo!

See, we have a hierarchy of values, whether or not we realize it consciously. Haven't you ever been in a situation where you felt like your priorities where out of line? Same thing. We are often at a loss to articulate why we feel out of kilter, but it is often because our basic values are not being met.

With Keith, Jim asked him if there might be another way to get both needs met simultaneously. He said that he and his wife both had bikes with seats on the back for kids (they were both little), and they could ride with them and get exercise at the same time. He was very enthusiastic about this, in his words, great new idea. Great new idea? It doesn't seem so groundbreaking when you stop and think about it, right? It seems kind of obvious, doesn't it? But often we don't see this type of thing for ourselves, but looking at the hierarchy of values and avoided states helps us to recognize any potential conflicts.

Conflicts between valued states and avoided states are very common, and in fact are natural. There is an inherent dynamic tension between these two. If you value peace, then you try to avoid conflict; if you value love, then you most likely avoid hate; if you value success, you try to avoid failure. But if you are going to have success, you will experience failure (recall Thomas Edison?). Many people do fail, but they don't allow their failures, their feelings of failure, or their fears of failure to stop them. That is the difference.

Let's stay with this example of success and failure, because you will certainly deal with this both with yourself and others. Any person who wants to be successful in anything, you name it, and he or she will fail far more times than they will succeed. Riding a bike, we all fell down far more times than we succeeded in staying up at first. Learning to walk, did you ever see a baby "get" walking on her first try? Conversely, did you ever see a baby get so frustrated and angry because she didn't walk perfectly that she quit? That she gave up and never tried again because she hadn't gotten it yet? Of course not. But have you ever seen non-babies do that? Not you personally, but maybe people you know? Many people value success, but they also want to avoid feelings of failure, or feeling like a failure. The problem comes when a person's fear or avoidance of failing prevents him from taking action and trying, or going through the necessary repetition of trial and error that it takes to master something.

This example might help to reinforce this concept:

There are professional racetracks open to the general public where you can learn to drive a NASCAR-style vehicle around a two and a half mile track at upwards of one hundred and fifty miles per hour. Can you imagine what that would be like? If you go, you are given everything you need to succeed, all the standard equipment, just like professional drivers. You receive a helmet, boots, gloves, and a fireproof suit, which hopefully you won't be needing. You are also paired up with a driving coach to help you be successful driving at this much higher level.

The driving instructors say that regardless of how talented a driver you are, though, you will never be great unless you learn to come out of a skid. They contend that at some point, you will go into a skid. It's unavoidable. No matter how powerful your machine is, or how quick you are, everybody at some time or another goes into a skid. There will be oil on the tarmac, or a car in front of you will spin out, or there will be a malfunction in your machine, and you'll go into a screeching, heart-stopping skid, more often than not right towards a wall, going over one hundred miles an hour.

What is common when going into a skid is to look directly at the wall, at what you fear, instead of focusing on where you want to go and getting back on track. To make sure you learn this lesson, you actually get to practice. It isn't theoretical, it's real life, "on the track" training. To make sure that you are fully prepared for a race, as you are rounding a curve, the pit crew has a radio-control that lifts one of your wheels, which will automatically put you into a skid. Of course, you are told that this will happen during the training before you go out on the track.

But prior advice or not, where do you think most people look when they go into the skid? Exactly. They look at the wall. Petrified, they focus directly on where they don't want to go, instead of looking at the track, where they would much rather be. Luckily, the helpful instructor is there to push your helmeted face in the direction of the track. Your hands, at that point still being attached to your body, also make adjustments, as your face is being twisted not too gently, so that the tires turn in the appropriate direction. Although not immediately, the tires do mercifully catch, you stop skidding, and probably at that point resume breathing, and you roar off at a somewhat slower pace around the track.

The interesting phenomenon about this training is that while many of the people that initially come to the tracks may have had dreams of racing cars, of taking it to the next level, they find that they are more afraid of the downside of what might happen, skidding and crashing, than they are excited about the possibilities that exist. As a result, they never tap into their potential as drivers. Instead of enjoying the full benefits of what they have, they creep along the track, content with not skidding, afraid of being out of control, reluctant to fail, or worse, not even trying again after the first frightening experience.

You'll never get where you want to be by focusing on what you fear.

In relation to what you have just learned, you see that they are more focused on states they want to avoid instead of those they want to achieve. The driving instructors tell them that they need to focus on what they want (what they value), instead of what they want to avoid (the wall).

Sometimes this fear is the result of actual failures and an individual's *personal reference* (remember this from **B**eliefs?), sometimes it is fear or hesitation based on other's input ("you'll never be able to do that" – *second-hand references*), and sometimes the feeling is completely based on *imagined references*. People hold themselves back because they want to avoid the feeling they think they will encounter in the future if they were to fail had they made the attempt. Fear of failure is one of the most common avoided states there is. Remember the statement, "we are what we think about most of the time?"

No one likes to be rejected, or unloved, or misunderstood, or virtually any of the avoided states that you can think of, and in a proper balance and perspective, it is not an issue. The challenge is that many times these are not in balance or a supportive perspective.

The most important role you can play in this step is to help another elicit these potential conflicts. Be wary of judging or trying to solve the conflict. Just help them to become aware of it. The next step should help them address any issues that arise.

I've never been afraid to fail.
-MICHAEL JORDAN

Identifying rules for determining Values and Avoided States

Jim had the opportunity to meet John McCormack back in 1993. An incredible visionary, and captivating speaker, John told a story that wonderfully illustrates the concept of **Rules** better than any other we have ever heard.

John McCormack is the author of *Self-Made in America*, and was Inc. Magazine's Entrepreneur of the Year in 1989. He is CEO of Visible Changes, a chain of hair salons in the southern United States that are extremely successful.

But John wasn't always so successful. Born into a working-class Irish-Catholic family in New York City, John had one of two options as a career, as he tells it. All the McCormack men either became priests or cops; it was one or the other. Since the celibacy part of the priesthood didn't appeal to him that much, he decided to become a police officer. So he joined the force at age 19, and began walking the streets of Brooklyn.

One day, a couple of years later, he got a call that changed his life forever. He was on foot patrol when he received word that there was an armed robbery in progress at a nearby neighborhood grocery store. John was close by, and he made tracks over to the store. With his weapon drawn, he entered the store, only to meet three men armed with sawed-off shotguns.

"Shoot him!" barked one of the men, apparently the leader.

No time to think, time was of the essence. Quickly, John responded, "Hey, wait a minute. Look, you're surrounded. There are cops all over the place. You shoot me, there is no way you will get out alive," he stated in what he hoped was a believable tone, since none of it was true.

They hesitated. Good sign. He continued, not wanting to lose his precarious advantage. "Besides, you probably didn't get very much anyway. I mean, come on, what did you get?"

"Twenty-eight bucks," one of the other men replied.

"Shut up!" screamed the leader. Apparently a two-word combination was this guy's preferred method of communication.

"Twenty-eight bucks?" John asked, quickly filling in the gap, not wanting the leader to repeat his earlier two-word order. "You're willing to die for twenty-eight bucks?" John said, no doubt asking himself the very same question. "Come on, it's over. Put your guns down, and I'll let them know you cooperated."

Through skillful negotiating, and a lot of good fortune, John made it out of there alive. But he was never the same. It really bothered him that he almost died over twenty-eight measly dollars. So he decided to take a leave of absence from the police force and figure out what he wanted to do with his life.

While he was considering his options, he and his brother got together to sell Christmas trees to make a little money. They rented a space in Manhattan, sold trees, and both made about $3,000. John took most of his money and invested in the stock market.

With what John describes as a little talent and a little luck, within a short period of time John parlayed that $3,000 into $100,000.

I think it was more like a *lot* of talent and a *lot* of luck. He got into the business of buying and selling stocks, and his own portfolio grew to $1,000,000 by the time he was twenty-five. He was a millionaire, replete with two limousines; one for him and one for his friends.

Well, as the saying goes, what goes up must come down. Within a short period of time, John lost that million, plus an additional $250,000 that he had borrowed figuring if he did it once, he could do it again. That didn't quite pan out, and he soon found himself $250,000 in debt, with no prospects of ever paying it back. He was not about to renege on his obligation, but the best job offer he got was for $18,000 a year. Even if he saved all that he earned, with a wife to support, there was just no way he could ever hope to pay back what he owed.

Totally despondent, he decided to take his own life so that at least his wife would collect the insurance money to live on. He said that his plan was swim out in the ocean until he couldn't swim any more. He was sitting on the beach trying to screw up his courage to go do it, when a voice called to him.

"Your ship's not gonna come in there."

John looked up at an elderly man shuffling towards him.

Before John had a chance to respond, the man continued, walking closer. "Your ship won't come in here. You gotta go to the harbor."

John figured him for a babbling fool. He had seen his share walking the beat. "What are you talking about?" John asked.

The man stopped, reached down and extended his hand. "My name is Abe. Is there something you want to tell me?" he said, in a calming and clear voice.

The question, and the timing, and Abe's energy all hit him at once. For some reason, John answered. All his pent-up frustrations and emotions came pouring out in his story. He told Abe about what happened on the police force, and about selling the Christmas trees, and how he made a million dollars, then lost it, and just after he told him that he was in the hole for two-hundred and fifty grand, Abe says, "You got fifty bucks?"

For cryin' out loud, John thought to himself, what a fool I am. The guy just wants a handout.

"You got fifty bucks or not?" Abe repeated.

"It's about all I have," John answered, "but…"

"Look," Abe continued. "I'll bet you five-hundred dollars to your little fifty, ten-to-one odds, that I can beat you in a foot race from here to that pier."

John was taken aback. The pier was about fifty yards away. John was twenty-six, and he figured Abe to be in his mid-seventies. "There's no way you can beat me in a race," John remarked.

"What, are you chicken? Afraid of losing to an old man?" Abe prodded.

"No, of course not." For a moment John must have wondered if Abe was an Olympian from 1908 or something. "I just don't want to take your money."

"Fat chance. You willing to do it?"

John was kind of annoyed, now. "Yeah, I'll do it," he replied. "I'll take your money if that's how you want it."

"Fine," Abe said. "But you have to put your feet in this." Abe took out a medium-sized canvas bag. "You still think you can do it?"

John paused for only a moment. "Yeah, I do." John put his feet in the bag.

"Great. Oh, one more thing." Abe spun John around. "You have to do it backwards," he shouted as he took off towards the pier.

John fell backwards, cursed, and got back up. By the time he got himself together again, Abe had already made it to the pier.

John was angrily taking out his wallet as Abe sauntered back. Abe put his hand lightly over John's. "Look, I didn't come here to take your money. Keep it."

John started to protest, then thought better of it.

"Think about what you learned here today. I'll meet you here Monday morning at eight am sharp. If you learned what I wanted you to learn, I'll consider working with you. If not, I never want to see you again." With that, Abe left. John scratched his head, and walked back to his car, his earlier mission forgotten, at least temporarily. Over the weekend he pondered the entire interaction with the old man.

Monday morning came, and Abe got right to the point. "Well, what did you learn?"

"I gave it a lot of thought," John replied. "I guess I learned that in any game, if you set up the rules, you can always win."

Abe smacked his forehead. A broad grin spread over his face. "Fantastic," he beamed. "I sent my sons to Ivy League schools, and they didn't get that. They are gonna waste my millions when I die." It just so happened that Abe was a multi-millionaire, a self-made man, an entrepreneur. He was walking the beach that day because he had just found out that his wife had cancer and had only a short time to live. He was distraught, and didn't know what to do, until he saw someone who looked like he was in even worse shape than himself.

For the next two years, Abe mentored John in the fundamentals of business. But as much as he learned, John said no lesson was more important than that first one.

In any game, if you set up the rules,
you can always win.
- JOHN MCCORMACK

STEP 4 Identify rules for determining Values and Avoided States

Take careful consideration and define the "rules" for each of your values, and for each of your avoided states. For example, if you value making a difference you can ask yourself questions such as:

- In what specific situations do I feel like I'm making a difference?
- How do I know when I have made or are making a difference?
- What does making a difference mean to me?
- What specifically has to happen in order for me to feel like I am making a difference?
- What is my definition of making a difference?

You can do the same thing with avoided states. Let's say you want to avoid feelings of being overwhelmed:

- In what types of specific situations do I tend to feel overwhelmed?
- What specifically has to happen for me to feel overwhelmed?
- How do I know when I am overwhelmed?
- What is my definition of overwhelm?
- What does being overwhelmed feel like to me?

Take careful note of the responses. Like Abe's race, who makes the decision who wins? Do other people have to do things for you to feel like you have won? If yes, then, who really controls your behavior?

Do your rules make it easy to feel bad, and hard to feel good? Many people set up their rules so it is very difficult to obtain positive feelings, and so easy to feel the negative feelings, all because their rules are set up in a way that does not support feeling very good. Ask yourself, "Do my rules support me or hold me back? Am I "winning" my own game?"

Any fool can make a rule, and every fool will mind it.

-HENRY DAVID THOREAU

STEP 5 Make changes in rules and hierarchies to align with objectives

Take a moment to reflect and review your list of hierarchies and rules; this may help to trigger your thought processes by asking yourself the following questions:

1. Looking at my list of values and avoided states, is the order consistent with who I want to be, how I want to act?

2. If not, how would I change the order? What impact would that have on me?

What things would I start doing? What things would I no longer do?

3. As I look at your list of rules, to what extent do they support me in "winning" according to my values?

4. To what extent might my rules hold me back, or prevent me from winning?

5. If appropriate, how might I change my rules to be more consistent with my values and avoided states hierarchy?

6. How would any of these changes impact my life, my performance, or my attitude?

This process can take quite a bit of time. Eventually, you will become more aware of values and avoided states in yourself, and through observation and a few well-placed questions, better understand what drives others.

Personally, we have worked with people on all three levels. Through experience we have found the most value when people truly commit to spending some time on this exercise on their own, and our role is one of providing a map of how to think about this. Afterwards, we review the responses together so that we both know what the individual wants and what they want to avoid.

STEP 6 Create action plans that are in alignment with your Values and Avoided States

This last step is vital. Many times people set goals that have very little to do with what they truly value in life, or they set goals that do not take into account what they want to avoid. Then they wonder why they aren't following through, and label themselves as lazy or undisciplined. Rarely is that the case. Generally, the problem is that people's goals have nothing to do with their value system or how they like to be reinforced.

Instead of expounding on this last step here, we would prefer to go into more detail in the chapters on **O**bjectives and **R**einforcement, since there we can share with you additional concepts and ideas which will help bring this all together.

Values
Key Points to Remember

1) A value is an emotional state; your values are in effect emotional states that are important to you.

2) We don't want things, such as money, relationships, material things or personal or professional achievement, as much as we desire the emotional states we think those things can give us.

3) Values provide a powerful motivating force for our behavior and the behavior of others. We all desire pleasure in our lives.

4) We also link pain to some emotional states. Since these are the states we try to avoid, we have termed them Avoided States.

5) We all move toward pleasure and away from pain. Some of us are driven   more by moving toward pleasure, some more by moving away from pain.

6) Sometimes we experience conflicts between or within pain and pleasure states.

7) We learned six steps to utilizing our Values effectively; they are:

   1) Identify all of your Values and Avoided States and list them on opposite sides of the paper.

   2) Organize the Values and Avoided States into a prioritized hierarchy.

   3) Identify any conflicts between or within your pain and pleasure states.

   4) Identify your rules for determining each of your Values and Avoided States

   5) Review and make changes in your rules and hierarchies to align and support your objectives (goals).

   6) Create action plans toward goals that are in alignment with your Values and Avoided States

The time is always right to do what is right.

-MARTIN LUTHER KING, JR.

Chapter Seven

Identity

As man imagines himself to be, so shall he be,
And he is that which he imagines.

-PARACELSUS

Who are you? How do you identify yourself? Such a simple question, isn't it? Or is it?

How important is an identity? How does one's identity affect behavior?

Do you think that an identity as a Protestant or a Catholic impacts the behavior of people in Ireland? Do you think that an identity as an Israeli or a Palestinian affect the behavior of people in the Middle East? Do you think that an identity as a member of a certain gang affects what kids will or won't do in cities across the world? Do you think having an identity as an American after the attacks of September 11th affected the way people acted? The answer to all of these questions is an undeniable yes.

On a more uplifting note, do you think that having an identity as a giver encourages certain behavior? You better believe it does. Do you think that identifying oneself as a winner enables one to dig down deep when the going gets tough? Absolutely.

Our sense of identity impacts us greatly. With an identity comes a code of conduct, a set of rules that govern behavior. These rules can be well known and published, or they can be unwritten, but understood. These rules can propel us to greatness, or can limit our potential. They can help us to achieve new heights, or they can drag us down and prevent us from reaching our potential. According to personal development expert Brian Tracy, each of us has a UHC or our Unique Human Capabilities. Your UHC is a statement of what you should do more of. It is your competitive advantage. He goes on to say, your unique combination of human qualities, skills and behaviors are so unique that the odds are 50 billion to one that there is someone out there just like you!

Consider the following identities, and think about the implications on behavior:

1. A U.S. Marine
2. A mom or dad
3. A Boy or Girl Scout
4. An honor student
5. A husband or wife
6. An IRS employee
7. The 1976 Springfield High School Homecoming Queen
8. A loser
9. A son or daughter
10. A vegetarian
11. An All-American athlete
12. A born-again Christian
13. An Olympic Gold Medalist

14. A health nut

15. A teammate

16. A neat freak

17. A Buddhist

18. A blind man

19. A deaf woman

20. A Mercedes owner

21. A classical pianist

22. A risk-taker

Each one of these identities has fairly specific connotations for behavior in our minds. Don't they in yours as well? If we ask someone to tell us about himself, he could mention any number of things with which he identifies: a son, father, grandson, husband, employee, engineer, runner, conservative, Republican, Catholic, neighbor, Princeton alumnus, anal-retentive, brother, gardener, computer geek, movie-aficionado, BMW-owner, singer, Billy Joel fan, rap-music hater, 3rd grade spelling bee champion, not a tree-hugger, future vice-president, and wine connoisseur. He could identify himself by his hobbies, his job, his relationships to other people, his likes, his dislikes, his religion, his philosophy, his political affiliation, his possessions, his past, his future, his strengths, his deficiencies, what he is, and what he isn't. Each can have a very specific impact on what he does or does not do, on what he allows himself to do or not do.

We make a living by what we get,
But we make a life by what we give.
- WINSTON CHURCHILL

Let's take a look at exactly what comprises your identity. Your identity has three components. The first is your self-concept. How we perceive ourselves, our concept of ourselves has a tremendous effect on the decisions that we make on a day-to-day basis. The term self-concept refers to those beliefs you have acquired that relate directly to you. Your self-concept determines the way you behave, and the way you perform at every activity.

The second component is your self-image. Your self-image is the picture you have of yourself. It is simply the belief system you have adopted about yourself and the images they produce. Your self-esteem is your third component; it is the emotional component of how you feel about yourself. More specifically, it is how you feel about the self-image your mind has created. It is not your physical image; it is your mental image, your inner mirror. Maxwell Maltz wrote about the importance of our self-image in his book ***Psycho-Cybernetics***. Maltz wrote, "The self-image is the key to human personality and human behavior. But, more than this, the self-image sets the boundaries of individual accomplishment. It defines what you can and cannot be. Expand the self-image and you expand the area of the possible. The development of an adequate, realistic self-image will seem to imbue the individual with new capabilities, new talents, and literally turn failure into success." Remember, you are who you think you are!

Consider the difference between two generals' concept of identity in the following:

Two generals are standing side by side, surveying the battlefield in front of them. Both are preparing for what will inevitably be a fierce fight. Heavy casualties cannot be avoided. The first general takes a deep breath in, and exhales forcefully and says to his assistant, "Get me my red cape."

The second general, confused, asks, "Why would you want to wear a red cape? You're setting yourself up to be a target."

The first general shakes his head, "That's not it at all. The reason I wear it is because I don't want my men to worry. If I am wounded in battle, then the blood will flow into the cape, and they will never know."

The second general nods his head in understanding, and says to his assistant, "Quick, go get me my brown pants."

Everybody has a number of possible identities; we aren't one-dimensional. We can identify to varying degrees with the various aspects of our lives. For example, there are people for whom being a certain race or religion is very important, while others might not even mention it if they were asked about how they might identify themselves.

In order to become more aware of your own identity, pay particular attention to how people identify themselves, at least in the moment. Consider the example *Mr. Cross Country*:

In this example Jim is speaking with a man we'll call Shaun about what motivates him to drive to California to study with a well-known martial arts teacher to accomplish certain goals he has in his life.

Jim's Winning Mind Set™ Example – Mr. Cross Country

I was teaching private Wing Chun Kung Fu lessons to Shaun. He was telling me about an upcoming trip out to California to train with a well known martial arts instructor.

"Now you drive out there, right?" I asked.

"Yeah, straight through."

"So what does it take you, five days?"

"Two. I don't stop," Shaun replied.

"Two days without stopping? Not even sleeping?"

Shaun shook his head. "Nope, straight through. It's tough, let me tell ya. But I couldn't take off that much time from work. I had to get back."

"How many times have you done this?" I inquired.

"There and back four times."

"So you have driven non-stop from New York to California eight times?"

"Yup," he answered.

"That is incredible. Not to downplay your situation at all, but man, how many people in the entire world do you think could do what you did?" Shaun, at least when he first came to see me, had an identity that was not empowering. He focused on how he had a dead-end job that didn't pay much, how he would never have enough money to own a house, how he lived with his mom, and how he couldn't open a martial arts school because he didn't have the finances. Now the truth was that he had so much going for him, yet in that moment, he was choosing to identify with certain aspects of his life that did not empower him. As I pointed out how unique this coast to coast excursion really is, I said to Shaun, "Do you realize how much discipline and stamina that takes? I get tired driving two hours non-stop. You drove for two entire days non-stop, and you not only did it once, you did it eight times. That is phenomenal."

"I dunno," he offered.

"Well I do. That is fantastic. You are Mr. Cross Country to me now", I cheered. "That's what I'm going to call you. Mr. Cross Country. If you can do that, if you can direct and control your mind and

body to be able to drive non-stop cross-country eight times, imagine what else you can do. Imagine what would happen if you directed that energy, that discipline and that focus towards other things? You're my driving hero, Mr. Cross Country, that's who you are."
Shaun laughed, "Yeah. I guess it was something I just really wanted to do."

"Wow, that's great. So how did you think about it to make it something you wanted to do? Did you picture your training? Because for you to be able to get all that money, which seems like it was a stretch for you..."

"Believe me it was."

"Yes it was, and for you to be able to get all that money, and to drive, you had to focus and direct your mind in a certain way, you had to not think about all the things that could have gone wrong going cross-country eight times. I'm impressed. I mean, what if your car broke down and you couldn't get back to work, or you were in an accident, or got lost, or any number of other things. For you to go ahead now and do what you really want to do, you used your mind in a very powerful way. I'm so intensely curious about what that was, because I bet you might just begin to imagine all of the things that you could do once you put that power of your mind to it- that power and focus and discipline that got you across the entire United States and back, from New York to LA, eight times- and I just can't help being so curious about what you will do next to get you closer to another important goal now, Mr. Cross Country."

Shaun smiled broadly, which was a marked difference from his visage when he first came in. "I just knew I wanted to do it. I just went from city to city, took it one step at a time. And I tell ya, Jimmy, there were some roads out there in the Rockies that were pretty hairy. I mean, there were no guardrails, and if you go off the road, it was a cliff straight down."

"That would ruin your whole day, huh?"

"You're not kidding."

"So did you picture your goal a certain way, or did you get a feeling?"

"I just knew it was something I had to do. So I took it one step at a time. But this school thing, man, I gotta get a license, and insurance, and a location, then a curriculum."

"So what would happen if you used the same approach that you did to go cross-country eight times here?" I asked. "If you looked at each step in the process of starting a school as if it were the next city you were traveling through, a benchmark? Because for you to be able to do what you did, you definitely chose to forget certain things, made a deliberate choice not to focus on those things that could hold you back, and instead be smart, do your homework, and move forward towards the completion of your goals. What do you think would happen if you used that powerful mind that way?"

"Yeah, I never really thought about it like that before."

"Well people better get out of your way when you do begin to think like that now, because you have done something that very few people can do, so you already know how to do it. Now you simply need to transfer that recipe over to a new situation called a school."

Jim didn't see him for a while after that; he was busy, and Jim was traveling. When they got together about two months later, Jim noticed that he looked in much better shape. "Hey, Mr. Cross Country. You're looking great. Looks like you lost some weight."

"Yeah, I've been working out more, watching what I have been eating. I've dropped twenty-five pounds."

Although he hadn't yet started a school, he spoke with a different attitude about his goal. Instead of expressing all the doubts and reasons why he couldn't do it as he had before, he was full of enthusiasm about sharing his knowledge with others and working towards getting a school, beginning with just a few students at a time, little by little working towards his goal.

In a half-kidding way, Jim wanted him to have a new identity, to relate to and remember a pretty phenomenal accomplishment so that he could use that identity to propel him forward in other areas as well. In my opinion, there are a whole lot of things *Mr. Cross Country* can do that Shaun could never pull off.

Each identity has implications, some beneficial, some not. Whereas identifying oneself as a Marine on the battlefield may be of great value (first to fight, never back down), this identity might not be as useful in a relationship. Perhaps focusing on an identity as a husband would work better.

Your Personal Attributes

What exactly makes a person perform better? It's hard to pinpoint exactly why one person excels far beyond his or her competitive peers. What winning combination do these *"Top Achievers"* possess that sets them apart? Why is the margin sometimes so pronounced? Why did Michael Jordan stand out? What allowed Gretzsky to dominate on the ice? Why does Mia Hamm seem to always be there when the ball is? What was the one quality that made Ali the seemingly unstoppable champ?

Let's not stop at sports, there must be one distinct feature that sets the top achievers in every field in a category of excellence that is exponentially unique! I've heard some say, it's genetics. But, is it? The world famous Martial Arts Master, Bruce Lee studied this same query. Lee was totally obsessed with the question of what made the superior athlete, technician, or warrior. Kevin began reading about Bruce Lee and studying with his protégé, Dan Inosanto over 20 years ago. This is where he first learned about the concept of concentrating on improving the defining **Qualities or Attributes** that made someone a top achiever or champion. Really, it is these attributes that create the combination that is superior.

> *"We are what we repeatedly do. Excellence, then, is not an act, but a habit."*
>
> - ARISTOTLE

What are attributes? Attributes are strengths that attribute to or help make up who you are, sort of like personal assets.

In order for us to have a clear distinction of our capability, aptitude and indeed our potential, we need to consider what our areas of strengths and weaknesses may be. In previous chapters we have identified some of our emotional strengths and weaknesses. We have also confirmed that our beliefs are in part relevant to our own perception of our strengths and deficiencies. These are some of the elements that contribute to the make-up of our identity, of who we are. But, it goes much deeper than that. Our attributes can be both psychological and physical in nature and can be naturally adopted skills and traits, or specifically learned and cultivated. We are of the belief that all attributes can be improved to some degree. It would also appear that certain attributes are absolutely crucial, if not critical, for any marked success in most given fields. When we have that critical combination of attributes, necessary to succeed in our chosen field of endeavor developed to a level outstanding to that of our competition, we increase our chances for success beyond what we would have ever believed possible!

Winning Mind Set™ Exercise – Identifying your attributes

Attributes are strengths that attribute to or help make up who you are, sort of like personal assets.

List four of your personal psychological attributes, which you feel you are strong at, and four that you feel you are weak at or would like to improve. Examples: integrity, focus, cheerfulness, persistence, clarity, flexibility, confidence, etc…

Strong   **Needs Improvement**

1. _____   1. _____
2. _____   2. _____
3. _____   3. _____
4. _____   4. _____

Now list two different methods you could use for continued development or improvement of each of these psychological attributes.

1. _____   1. _____
                  2. _____
2. _____   1 _____
                  2. _____
3. _____   1. _____
                  2. _____
4. _____   1. _____
                  2. _____
5. _____   1 _____
                  2. _____
6. _____   1. _____
                  2. _____
7. _____   1. _____
                  2. _____
8. _____   1. _____
                  2. _____

List four of your personal physical attributes which you feel you are strong at and four which you feel you are weak at or would like to improve. Examples: balance, flexibility, strength, speed, timing, coordination, etc…

Strong	**Needs Improvement**
1. _____	1. _____
2. _____	2. _____
3. _____	3. _____
4. _____	4. _____

Now list two different methods you could use for continued development or improvement of each of these physical attributes.

1. _____
                     1. _____
                     2. _____

2. _____
                     1 _____
                     2. _____

3. _____
                     1. _____
                     2. _____

4. _____
                     1. _____
                     2. _____

5. _____
                     1 _____
                     2. _____

6. _____
                     1. _____
                     2. _____

7. _____
                     1. _____
                     2. _____

8. _____
                     1. _____
                     2. _____

How can you use this?

First you must identify what qualities the most outstanding people in your chosen endeavor possess that make them outstanding. Now, write these qualities/attributes on a sheet of paper. Now investigate your personal qualities and areas of necessary improvement introspectively with absolute honesty. Where do you stand? What areas can you improve in? You are on the way to making some of the most important distinctions for improving your future success that you have ever made in your LIFE!

Your Critical Success Factors

Let's take this a step further. According to studies conducted at Harvard University, there are usually four or five Critical Success Factors (CSF's) in everything you do. These CSF's are things you must do order to be successful in what you set out to accomplish in any given field or endeavor.

If you have a weakness in any one of your Critical Success Factors, it can bring all of your strong CSF's down dramatically. Critical Success Factors are, in effect, more than just attributes, they are essential qualities.

An example of a CSF in basketball is cardiovascular endurance. You may be a great passer, and shooter and understand the fundamentals perfectly, but if you are tired and can't keep up with the game… you're done. We have seen this factor be totally apparent over and over in combative sports, such as boxing. Many times it is not necessarily the better technician who wins in wrestling, boxing and Thai Boxing, but the more conditioned athlete.

Another example we can use is in business. Any banker will tell you that less than 3% of all small businesses succeed within the first year. The major reason for **failure** is under-capitalization of the investment in starting the business. Therefore, one of the critical success factors in starting and successfully running any business is ample working capital. It doesn't matter how knowledgeable you are or how good you are at the skills pertaining to the business. It doesn't even matter how great your market is. Without the Critical Success Factor of money, you will not succeed.

Winning Mind Set™ Exercise – Identifying CSF's

Take a moment to reflect on the critical success factors in your field or in any area you may feel challenged. Identify them and rate them from 1-5 as accurately and honestly as possible.

1-being poor
2- being below adequate
3- being adequate
4- being excellent
5- being exceptional

CSF   **Rating**

How is this crucial to your to your performance? The more exceptional your CSF's, the greater your success will be in your effort!

The Identification Card

In one paragraph, create an Identity Card for yourself. In that paragraph, chronicle all those aspects of yourself that you feel are most important to you:

Now review your list, and then write out (or discuss) the answer to the question, "What made you identify with these aspects of yourself so strongly?"

Implications of Identity

**List out (or discuss) the implications of such an identity on
your behavior. What does having such an identity allow you
to do? Prevent you from doing? What does this "identity"
do or not do?**

**Review (or discuss) your findings. Are there any unintended
negative consequences to some of your identities? What are
the benefits of identifying strongly with certain aspects of
who you are?**

The Winner provides an excellent example of this concept of Identity in practice:

Jim's Winning Mind Set™ Example – The Winner

I once worked with a very gifted athlete, and he identified very strongly with being a winner. While that identity was useful in many ways, it had its drawbacks as well. As a winner, he had no time for helping the younger or less experienced players on his team. After all, he was all about winning, not about helping others to develop (this was primarily an individual sport). Anyone who was not geared towards being supportive of his success was of little value to him.

He would also get extremely frustrated and tense if another person on his team got the better of him in practice. As such, he would only practice with people he could beat, and he actually had a competitive intensity, almost a disdain towards his teammates that was generally reserved for opponents.

So while winning was certainly important to him, his primary focus on his identity as a Winner prevented him from also seeing himself as a Learner, a Teammate, a Friend, a Son, and a Teacher to the younger or less skilled athletes.

I asked him, "What does being a winner mean to you? In other words, what do you do or not do because you are a winner?"

He thought for a moment. "I train really hard, I can't let up."

"That seems like a good thing that you train really hard. That certainly helps you to win. What else?"

"I have a certain intensity. I hate when people dog it," he said.

"Meaning take it easy?" I asked.

"Yeah. I can't stand that."

"Okay, what else do you do or not do because you are a winner?"

"I don't do drugs or alcohol, none of that. I don't party."

"Those are positive qualities, huh?" I remarked.

He nodded his head.

"What about being a winner is not as good?"

He frowned. "What do you mean?"

"Well, as a winner you have certain rules, a certain code of conduct that guides your behavior, that dictates what you do or don't do. You may not be aware of it, but it's there."

He thought for a while. "Well, I guess I have a pressure to always be the best. Sometimes that isn't so great. I mean, I don't feel like I can ever relax and just have fun, that it always has to be serious."

"What does not feeling like you can relax and have fun do?" I asked.

"It's like I can't just goof off sometimes."

"And what would just goofing off sometimes be like?"

"I don't know. It would make it more fun, I guess."

"And if it were more fun?"

"I guess I would like it more. Now, I can't see doing this in college. It's too much pressure," he said.

"It's too much pressure," I repeated. "So let me ask you something. What if, instead of thinking of yourself as primarily a winner, you thought of yourself as a learner? What would that be like?"

"I'm not sure I follow you."

"What if, when you went to practice, you said to yourself that you are here to learn, not to win, or perform, but learn; and you didn't have to be a learner every day, but maybe once a week you focused on being a learner. How would that be?"

He pondered that idea. "I think it might be fun. I could try stuff out that maybe I was hesitant to before."

"Sometimes when people identify so strongly with something, they aren't willing to try new things. But if they get an opportunity to be someone else, even for a little while, they are free to explore new areas that can be very educational."

He nodded his head, but said nothing.

"What if you thought of yourself as a teacher? How would that change what you did or didn't do?" I asked.

He raised his eyebrows. "Oh, it would be a lot different. I would probably help out with the other guys on the team. I would learn more techniques so that I could help everyone out, even if I didn't use that certain move myself."

"Okay, so you would learn more. What else?"

"I guess I would be interested in how other people learned, and what worked or didn't work in terms of teaching them."

"That would be interesting, wouldn't it?" I replied. "How might that help you?"

Again, he hesitated before answering. "I guess it would force me to look at things from different angles, and help me to learn things in greater detail because I would have to teach it."

"What if, in addition to seeing yourself as a winner- which supports you in being healthy and taking care of yourself, and trying hard- you also saw yourself as a learner, and a teacher- so that you felt more relaxed and carefree, and were willing to try new things, and you also helped others learn new things, and in fact learned more deeply about a whole series of things. What would that be like?"

"It would be great," he said, nodding.

"It would be great, and you may even begin to wonder what other identities you could begin to focus on, like a teammate, that could help you even more, so as you go home you can begin to think about these things and become even more than you were before, in whatever way makes the most sense to you now."

One's identity is a combination of personal values, and team, group, cultural and societal norms. Just as one's personal value system has inherent within it states that we work towards and states we want to avoid, so do team, group, cultural, and societal influences; just as we have rules for our values and avoided states, so too do teams, groups, cultures, and societies have expectations and norms for behavior.

Understanding the influence of these larger groupings and the interaction with, support of, or conflict with personal values can be quite beneficial, and represents another powerful tool in your *Winning Mindset™* toolkit.

Identity
Key Points to Remember

1)   Your identity has a powerful impact on our behavior.

2)   Your identity has three components.
   * Your self-concept
   * Your self-image
   * Your self-esteem

3)   We are not just one entity; our identities are based on the various facets of our lives.

4)   In order for us to have a clear distinction of our identity, we need to consider what our areas of strengths and weaknesses may be.

5)   What is your ID? What are the implications of such an identity on your behavior? What does having such an identity allow you to do? Prevent you from doing? What does this "Identity" do or not do?

6)   One's identity is usually a combination of personal values, and team, group, cultural and societal norms.

We lift ourselves by our thoughts,
We climb upon our vision of ourselves.

-ORISON SWETT MARDEN

Chapter Eight

Objectives

Undertake something that is difficult; it will do you good.
Unless you try to do something beyond what you have
already mastered, you will never grow.

-RONALD E. OSBORN

It has been stated that "Goal setting is the Master skill of success". It has also been said that setting and achieving pertinent goals is perhaps the single most important element to our personal growth and success. What is a goal or an objective? An objective is like a target really. If you currently have clear, written goals to lead you forward, you are part of a very unique group. You are aiming at the center of the bull's eye of your target. You are in the top 3% of people who have high aspirations about their personal achievement.

As amazing as it sounds only 3% of North Americans have clear, written goals. In addition, only 10% have goals committed to memory. This would be like aiming at the outside rim of your target. Committing goals to memory is not an adequate way to clearly focus on your objective. Something truly amazing happens when you write down your goals. It's as if they are beginning to actually process in your mind the moment your pen hits the page. Imagine if only 3% have written goals and only 10% have mental goals, what about the other 87%? Well 87% of North Americans have NO GOALS, what so ever! Not only that, out of that 87%, 60% are content if they can just "make it through life", the remaining 27% of people would prefer to have something for nothing.

Kevin's Winning Mind Set™ example – The Swimmer

Once, during a check up, my doctor asked me about the coaching I have developed a reputation for.

"So, what's this thing you do?" Mike asked.

"What thing is that Doc?" I answered teasingly.

"This performance enhancement stuff you do with some of the athletes you work with?" Mike said.

"Why Doc, what do you have on your mind?" I inquired.

Mike looked me in the eye and said with a twinkle, "I'm thinking about entering the NY Empire State Games in swimming."

"Wow, Mike that's great, you used to compete in swimming? When was that?"

"Oh, when I was in high school." Doctor Mike replied.

"Wow, that was a long time ago, what'd you have in mind?"

"I'd like to enter six events, just to see how I'd do." Mike said, half-heartedly.

"Then why bother?" I said, sensing the apprehension in Mike's voice. Mike stared at me in disbelief at his remark. Was this the attitude of a top coach?

I continued, "If you want to see how you'll do, why not just have your times checked, then compare them to the people that would swim in your class. You're way too busy to do something as time consuming as this **just to see how you'll do**. Doc, you have a booming practice, a beautiful wife and a huge family. You're a very successful, very busy man. Mike, it takes dedication and time to swim at that level, so I mean really unless you're going all the way, don't bother." I said as I pierced Mike with my gaze.

Mike looked at me and a grin appeared, "Oh, I get it, we've started already haven't we?"

"Mike, you're an archer right, you shoot a bow? So, tell me when you aim for the target, do you always hit the Bull's Eye?" I inquired.

"No" Mike laughed.

"Well, what if you aim for the Bull's Eye do you usually hit the target?" I continued.

"Most of the time…yes" Mike said a little puzzled.

"What if you aim for the center of the Bull's Eye, aren't you much more likely to hit the center ring? Doc, I would love to work with you, but if you're going to aim, aim for the GOLD, OK?"

I set up a time when we could meet and I could work with Mike. Once I created a sense of total commitment for success in Mike we began. In the one on one session I had with Mike we zeroed in on a success plan. I then helped Mike establish a reason for him to work on his swimming goal that was congruent with his values. Purpose or "The Why" is always more powerful than any goal. We did a series of personal visualization history searches and came up with a time when Mike was in the top of his class. I then used that past event as an emotional connection for Mike to tap into prior to his future swimming events. Finally, I had Mike pick an anchor series that was congruent with his faith, his family and his goal.

I didn't see Doc for a while but the next time I went for a check up, I asked him, "Hey Doc, how'd you do at the Empire State

Games?"

"Well, I used your techniques and I did pretty good. I entered five events and took three bronze and two silvers."

"That's great, don't worry there's always next year for the Gold", I smiled.

Note: Mike also took 3 silver and 2 bronze medals in 2003 and 4 gold and 2 silver in the 2004 Empire Games. In addition to winning 16 medals in 3 years at the Empire State Games, Mike also showed his eight-year-old son, who then used it to qualify in swimming for the State Finals.

Thank you very much for my lesson prior to the 2002 Empire State Games competition. The advice and techniques you taught were responsible for my profound success, far above what I thought could be achieved. In one race, I was seeded 7th in my age group. My qualifying time was bettered by 30 seconds (in the 200 meter event) and I ended up in third place. My 5 medals (3 bronze/2 silver) from those 5 events were a far greater accomplishment than I ever deemed possible. Thanks for your sage advice, and I am forever grateful for your service. -Dr. Michael C. Kennedy Master's Swimming Participant and Gold Medalist

We all have dreams. But in order to make the dreams into reality, it takes an awful lot of determination, dedication, self-discipline, and effort.
-JESSE OWENS

One of our core beliefs is that the only thing constant is change. Changes affect every single aspect of our lives. For most people change is very frightening, it threatens their stability, and there is an almost primal desire deeply rooted in most people to avoid change of any kind. This fear of change is as old as the history of human development itself. The underlying reason for this fear is it is **an unknown**, and a trait of human behavior, is to be primarily fearful of the unknown. This is one of the reasons that having goals is so important. Having a direction, and a progression toward the accomplishment of an objective gives us a feeling of familiarity and, vision and control. Goals help us to take control of the direction of change in a positive and empowering way. Your goals assure you that the changes you make in your life are in the direction you want to go and if well planned give you the progression to achieve those changes.

If you don't know where you're going,
any road will take you there!
-BRIAN TRACY

You may have heard of the acronym SMART for setting goals or objectives:

Specific
Measurable
Achievable
Realistic
Time-bound

We think that is an excellent start. We added two more categories, since being SMART is good, but being SMARTER is better.

Specific
Measurable
Achievable
Realistic
Time-bound
Emotionally Satisfying
Relevant

Specific – objectives ought to be as specific as possible. Instead of an ambiguous objective such as "increase sales", "lose weight", "win more", or "become better at presentations", the objectives should be *very specific*. They should also be stated *in the positive* (as opposed to "I *don't* want to look and feel this way any more), *personal* (what the individual needs to do, not what other people should do) and in the *future desired state* (I will weigh 160 pounds as opposed to I will lose 20 pounds).

1. What specifically will you do?

2. When will you do it?

3. What is your end goal?

According to Jack Canfield, W. Clement Stone used to write his goals on the back of his business card and place it in his wallet where he would see it every time he opened it. Hilton wrote his goal of owning a hotel, similar to the Waldorf Astoria, and placed it on the mirror where he could see it every day while working as a busboy at the Waldorf.

Actor Jim Carrey wrote himself a check for acting services rendered for $10,000,000 in 1990 and dated it for Thanksgiving 1995. He placed the check in his wallet and carried it around with him for years. By 1995 he was paid $20 million per picture.

Measurable – This helps you to keep track of your progress. Writing it down, as simple as it seems, helps you to solidify in your mind a sense of purpose and progress. You can also review results for gains, losses, and plateaus in order to understand when a new approach may be warranted.

1. How will you know when you have achieved your objective?

2. What measurements will you use?

3. What system will you use to keep track of your progress?

One of our favorite methods of tracking our progress is by writing in a journal. Kevin writes a journal for each major project. He carries the journal with him and tracks the progress of the project as it develops momentum.

Achievable – Establish goals that are achievable in the time frame that is specified. Set mini-goals along the way that are specific, measurable, and achievable. This way you can sense some progress, and also determine if you are on or off track. Whereas running a marathon may not seem achievable for someone who has never run before, setting a goal to run a marathon in two years, and then starting out with smaller, more "bite-size" goals will make it seem possible.

**Most goals, if viewed in their entirety,
would seem daunting.
Set your mind on your objective,
then work at it little by little.**

---

1. What mini-goals or steps seem to make the most sense for you?
2. What can you do today? This week? This month towards the achievement of your goal?
3. What length of time motivates you the most?

Realistic –Would anyone have thought that the Wright brothers' goal of flying was realistic? What about Thomas Edison's goal of inventing the electric light bulb? Did anyone think that a human being could run a mile in less than four minutes until Roger

Bannister did? Never limit your imagination, for there is an awesome power there.

> **The only way to discover the limits of the possible**
> **is to go beyond them into the impossible.**
>
> -ARTHUR C. CLARKE

We've seen people achieve things that, frankly, absolutely amazed us. We didn't think they could have ever pulled it off. But they did. Rather than limit their goals, we ask them about their beliefs supporting that goal. We would make sure that they felt a sense of certainty in their entire system, either through personal references, second hand references, or imagined references.

1. Given other things that you are doing, what are you willing to commit to?
2. How will you fit this into your current schedule?
3. What might you have to stop doing in order to fit this in?

Time-bound – Just as objectives should be measurable and specific, they also need to be time-bound to be most effective. Someone once said that goals are just dreams with a deadline. Establish goals that have specific timelines associated with them. Again, have the goals broken down into achievable chunks, with dates assigned to each. It is incredible how something like a deadline gets you to focus on your goal.

1. When does it make the most sense for you to / do you see yourself achieving your goal?

2. When does it make the most sense for you to / do you see yourself achieving your sub-goals?

Emotionally satisfying – Sometimes people set goals and achieve them, only to say, "Is that it? Is this all there is? I thought it would feel different." Make sure you are aware of what attaining your goal means to you emotionally. Ask yourself what it means to achieve your goals, and imagine what it would be like in the future to have already achieved them.

1. What feelings will working towards this goal give you?
2. How will it feel to achieve your goal?
3. What will you have gained by working towards this goal? (this statement acts as if the goal has already been achieved)
4. What will you have gained by achieving this goal? (same for this one)

Relevant – This is the one element that gets overlooked the most often. For goals to be truly inspiring, they need to be linked to and congruent with your value system. If a goal helps you to fulfill your most important values according to your rules, and helps steer clear of avoided states, then that goal is highly likely to be achieved. The more you link a goal to multiple values, and see how achieving that goal helps you to stay away from avoided states, the better.

1. How does working towards this goal and achieving it fit in with your overall values?
2. What about working towards this goal and achieving it is so important to you?

I'm a firm believer in goal setting, step by step. I can't see any other way of accomplishing anything.

-MICHAEL JORDAN

There is a unique cycle that occurs when we predicate goals that are in alignment with our values. As you work toward your value driven objective you feel totally natural in your pursuit and once this goal is achieved, your values are satisfied and supported by your accomplishment, the result of your efforts. Therefore, your goals support your values and your values in turn support you in the direction of your goals.

Let's look at the example ***Working Out*** to give an illustration of these principles:

Jim's Winning Mind Set™ example – Working Out

A woman asked me for help setting up an exercise routine. She had enjoyed working out a number of years back, but had gotten out of the habit. She wanted to lose about thirty pounds, and said she was excited about exercising again and getting back into shape.

I scheduled some time with her over lunch one day. "Mary, I can certainly help you put together a routine for exercising. That is easy. You could also pick up one of hundreds of books or magazines to get advice on an exercise routine, so it's not difficult to obtain the knowledge about how to work out", I said.

She agreed.

"Knowing how to exercise doesn't guarantee that you will do it on a consistent basis, that you will feel good about it and find it enjoyable, because figuring out what motivates you, or prevents you from doing it is something completely different, isn't it?"

"Yes", Mary agreed.

"In fact, I bet with the knowledge you have right now, you could go work out, couldn't you?"

She confirmed, and said that she belongs to a gym.

"So you could, then, go right now. So do you?" I asked.

"Does it look like I do?" she joked.

"What prevents you from going right now?"

"I don't have the time."

"Do you lie about other things too?" I mused.

Mary laughed.

"When people tell me that they don't have the time to do something, what they are really saying is that what they say they want to do isn't as important to them as what they are currently doing right now. If it was, they would do it, they would find the time. So you can give me all the excuses you want about why you aren't exercising, including that you don't have the time, but you and I both know that isn't the real reason, that if you really wanted to do it, you would do it. Am I right?"

She nodded her head. "You're right."

"So it is completely up to you whether or not you want to spend the time exercising. You did ask for help, though, so at least at some level it seems that you want to exercise. Is that true?" I pressed.

"Oh yeah, I do."

"Okay, so what really prevents you from going to exercise?"

"I don't know," Mary said.

"And if you did know what would you say?" I persisted.

"The place that I go is mostly guys who are in great shape. Where I used to go there was more women."

"And that means?"

"I didn't feel as self-conscious."

"Because of ...?"

"My weight," Mary replied.

"So if it weren't for your weight, if you were in great shape, the shape that you wanted to be in now, would the fact that guys were at the gym prevent you from exercising?"

Mary shook her head. "No, I wouldn't care."

"You wouldn't care, that's right, so why not?" I asked.

"I'd be confident," she answered.

"And when in your life did you feel the most confident?"

Mary paused for a moment before answering. "From about 1991 to 1995. I was working out. I was in great shape, and about thirty pounds lighter. I knew I could do anything. I could deal with anything." As she spoke about that period of time, she straightened up in her chair, put her shoulders back, and smiled.

"So I noticed that as you were talking about your experiences back then, feeling confident, you changed your body. Did you realize what you did?" I remarked.

"I sat up straighter," she said.

"You sat up straighter. Yes. Anything else?"

"I don't know. My face probably changed."

"That's right, your face did change. You smiled, and you relaxed the area between your eyebrows. So your body knows exactly what it feels like to be confident, doesn't it? It already knows what to do."

Mary nodded her head.

"So if you will, I'd like you to think back to a specific time when you were working out and you felt absolutely confident. A very specific memory of a time you felt absolutely confident. Can you go back there now?"

"Yes." Mary said.

"Yes, and where are you?"

"I'm in the gym, and it's summer, and I have a great tan, and I'm wearing red shorts and a gray T-shirt that's kind of tight. I can't believe I'm telling you this."

"That's right, and you are feeling great, aren't you, and feeling great, feeling confident, not too hard to do, considering you are in great shape. And as you are working out and feeling so confident now, how are you holding yourself? What are you doing with your body?" I asked.

Mary straightened up even more, held her chin up high, breathed fully, and smiled a self-satisfied grin.

"Looks pretty good to me," I continued. "So what would you do to feel twice as confident as you do even now? What would you do with your body, your shoulders, your neck, your face, your eyes, your breathing, to feel twice as confident as you do right now as you are in that gym, all tan, feeling great?"

Mary took an even deeper breath, her eyes narrowed slightly, and she relaxed the muscles of her neck.

"That's right. That's right. Breathing fully, head up, smiling like that, feeling confident now. And feeling this way, confident, how do you feel about exercising?" I asked.

"Great. I love it."

"How about exercising right now, today?"

"Great."

"So even with all the other commitments that you have, and the fact that you are thirty pounds heavier, how do you feel about exercising now?" I inquired.

Mary laughed. "I feel great. I want to do it."

"You feel great, and you want to do it. What about all the guys there?"

Mary laughed again. "It doesn't matter."

"It doesn't matter, does it? And it doesn't matter because?"

"Because I feel great."

"You feel great and you feel confident. So what is feeling confident and relaxed and great? How do you get into that state? You have a certain recipe for doing that, don't you? What is it? What do you do with your body?"

Mary explained what she did with her shoulders, head, face and breathing.

"And you have so many memories of feeling confident that can help you, of feeling great, and you can go back there at any time and remember those feelings now, can't you? Yes, you can, and you can use your recipe of confidence, too. Your memories and your recipes, feeling great and confident now. That's right."

Mary beamed. "I'm going to do it. Starting Sunday. I'll start slow, do a little bit at a time, and I'll get there."

"What about all the other stuff you have to do, though? Why will you do this now?" I asked.

Mary shook her head. "The other stuff I'll deal with. I feel so much better when I exercise, about everything. It's important. I feel better about myself, I have more energy, I feel better with other people. I'm going to do it."

"Okay, so specifically, what are your goals?" I inquired.

"I'm going to go to the gym twice a week to start."

"Great, when are you going to go?"

"I'll go Wednesdays after work, and on Saturday," Mary answered.

"Great. When on Saturday, just to be completely anal about this," I teased.

"I'll say. Uh, let's say two o'clock. By then I'll have all my errands done."

"Okay, Wednesdays after work and Saturdays at two you are going to go to the gym. How long will you exercise and what specifically will you do?"

"Let's see. I'll go on the treadmill for twenty minutes to get started, then I'll do a complete circuit for weight lifting, and that should take about twenty or twenty-five minutes, so about forty-five minutes total." Mary gleemed.

"Okay, forty-five minutes total, and do you know how to do the weights?"

"Yeah, oh yeah," she answered.

"Great. And so getting there is your first goal, and you have set that. So what specific goals do you have for weight loss? You said you wanted to lose thirty pounds?"

She smiled. "I did, didn't I?"

"Yes, afraid so."

"Yeah, thirty pounds."

"Okay, so I'd like you to write down your desired weight in a notebook where you will look at it. You don't have to show me." I laughed.

"Don't worry," she said, laughing.

"But keep it handy as your target weight. And how often will you weigh yourself?"

"Oh no, this is serious, isn't it?" she whined.

"Only if you want it to be," I replied.

"No, I do, I do. On Saturdays I'll weigh myself at the gym."

"Great. And what is your goal for being at your ideal weight? When would you like to do that in a healthful way?"

"I think within nine months to a year. I put it on over time, and I don't want to rush it. I think nine months to a year." Mary verified.

"Okay, great. So should we say nine months, or a year, or somewhere in between? It's up to you when you want to get to your ideal weight, either within nine months or take the entire year. Which seems better?"

Mary paused. "Well, let's say that I will be at my ideal weight plus five pounds within nine months, and then definitely at my ideal weight within a year."

"Sounds like a plan," I said. "One thing you may want to consider is having multiple mini-goals that lead up to your major goal. You could have your first goal of making it to the gym twice a week to start, and then you can figure out what you want to do in terms of eating more healthfully as well, and have daily, weekly or monthly goals, whichever seem to motivate you best. Some people like daily goals that they can check off, like a to-do list, other people like longer range goals. You can decide which approach works best to motivate you to achieve your goal."

"That's a good idea," she said, taking notes.

"And so tell me, Mary, what will exercising and being at your ideal weight mean to you? What benefits will you get?"

"I'll have more energy, for one thing, and I'll feel better about myself."

"That's right, and by having more energy and feeling better

about yourself, what will that enable you to do?" I asked.

"I'll have more energy to help other people."

"And that's important to you, isn't it?", I concluded.

She nodded her head, "Yes, it is."

"So by taking action in certain areas, you can help other people and help yourself. How will that make you feel?"

"It would feel great."

"So do something with me, if you will. I want you to close your eyes, and I want you to imagine yourself one year from now, sitting in that same chair, feeling relaxed and confident, and full of energy, being at your ideal weight now, and feel what it feels like to have all that energy, and know that you have that energy to help others and to help yourself, and knowing that you can feel as confident and energetic as you want now, just relax as you sit there and feel all of those good feelings, and see yourself going to the gym, maybe wearing a tight T-shirt and shorts, and how it feels to look and feel good, and you may even get noticed by other people, and that can feel good too, can't it? And really congratulate yourself for following through on your goals day by day, having more energy and confidence and fun, too, right? Because it is fun to be feeling great and active now, and as you breathe in deeply feel a sense of warmth and accomplishment and energy and gratitude for all that you have been able to do for yourself and others over the last year, and as you take another deep breath in and exhale out you can open your eyes feeling confident and relaxed and energized as you do what you want for you and others."

She opened her eyes slowly, and smiled. "I'm going to do it."

"I know you will," I said. I extended my hand, and shook hers firmly.

Read the example again and see how Jim used The Winning
Mind Set™ to help Mary be clearer about her objectives.

*I feel that the most important step in any major
accomplishment is setting a specific goal. This enables
you to keep your mind focused on your goal and off
the many obstacles that will arise while you're striving
to do your best.*

-KURT THOMAS

Focus is a major key to your success

One of the qualities that distinguishes high achievers in
all areas of life is their ability to focus with clarity, persistence and
definition beyond the average person. It is this absolute razor sharp
imagery that will bring you success. Whatever you consistently think
about and focus on, you move towards and eventually will become.

When Kevin works with children in the martial arts, his greatest
challenge is to capture the focused attention of his adolescent students
for the duration of the lesson. One of the analogies he uses to explain
the importance of focus is this: "You can have the most expensive
cameras made and purchase the very best film. You can also have the
most incredible subject, an expansive canyon, a breathtaking sunset,
a beautiful, bright flower, or the face of someone you love very much.
Now, if you begin to take that picture and your camera is not in focus,
what do you get? Your camera will record an image that is blurry and
hard to see. You have an image that is not memorable or sharp. This is
what your mind is like. In order to get a sharp, long lasting image of

what you've seen or learned, you must focus your mind!

Now it is up to you, do you want a box of blurry, unfocused pictures of what you've learned or an album of beautiful, sharp memories? Your focus is the key. The sharper your memories are the clearer they will be when you play them over and over in your mind." This example is so effective that students have often mentioned the "focus concept" to Kevin many years later and how they remember the day he explained it to them.

Another concept Kevin uses to gain the improved focus necessary for sharp mental imagery and a fast learning curve is this: when you play, think about nothing else. Immerse yourself 100% in the fun and play. Don't think about school, don't let your homework or chores around the house enter your mind. Play 100%! When you work, work. Don't let yourself become distracted, daydream about vacation or playing with your friends. Work and focus totally on your work. By using this simple technique, you will improve your work production, time will fly by and you will absolutely astound yourself. You'll have less stress, more total focus, better work skills and more enjoyment when you play. What a simple yet amazing concept.

Don't let your dreams be dreams
-JACK JOHNSON
MUSICIAN/SONGWRITER

Filling Your Jar

During class one day, a college professor brought out a jar and a small pile of rocks. His analogy was that the jar was the time we had available and the rocks were the tasks we needed to complete. After placing the rocks in the jar he asked the students if the jar was full. When the students responded with a unified "yes", he brought out some gravel and poured it into the jar, filling the gaps between the larger rocks. He then asked the class if the jar was full now. The students now wise to the analogy, all replied "no".

The teacher then brought out a bag of sand and poured some into the jar, filling yet more gaps in the vessel. At this point the attendants felt certain that the jar must be full. Once again the teacher reached down and this time bringing a pitcher of water up onto the table, began to pour some of the liquid into the now apparently full jar until it was at the brim of the jar.

He turned his attention to the curious students and asked, "What is the lesson we learned from the demonstration today?" One of the brightest students replied confidently, "We always have more time than we think." The teacher smiled and said, "No, the only way you will fit the biggest tasks in your schedule is to apply them first!"

World-renowned personal development and business consultant, Brian Tracy say's, "Every morning when you get up eat a live frog! At that point in time there will be no doubt that this will be the most difficult thing you've accomplished today!" Brian is, of course, speaking metaphorically. Basically, try to accomplish the tasks that are the most overwhelming, the one's you are most afraid to start because of their sheer immensity or your emotional connection and negative association you have to them.

You are always free to choose what to do first,
what to do second,
and what not to do at all.
-BRIAN TRACY

How can you use this? Always work on your largest tasks first, if you start with your simple, small tasks, they will continue to accumulate as your day progresses and you will be majoring in minor job tasks all day long. We want to accomplish those things that most contribute to our success in the areas we work in. Trust us, the small tasks will still be there when you are done with the major job task! Use the end of your day, when you're less productive to clean up the small details.

Three Rules of work:
1. Out of clutter, find simplicity.
2. From discord, find harmony.
3. In the middle of difficulty lies opportunity.
-ALBERT EINSTEIN

The Amazing potential of setting and achieving one's goals

Have you heard the story of John Goddard? John Goddard was a famous explorer and world adventurer, deemed by *Reader's Digest* to be the *real* Indiana Jones. Goddard's amazing story was featured in *Life* magazine in 1972.

At fifteen John was fed up with adults telling him what he

could and couldn't do with his life. John heard his grandmother say that she wished she had done more when she was younger. John swore he would not feel the same about his life and that he would experience life to the fullest.

He decided to make a list of "lifetime goals" that would astonish even the most adventurous. A few of his 127 challenging lifetime written goals included: the seventeen mountains he wanted to climb, including Mount Everest, the Matterhorn and Mount Kenya. In addition, he wanted to explore eight of the world's great rivers, which included the Amazon, the Nile and the Congo Rivers. It was his goal to learn to fly a plane and to circumnavigate the earth, which he accomplished four times. He wanted to travel the world, studying the cultures of people of twelve different countries, some of which included the jungles of Borneo and Brazil, as well as the arid region of Sudan and the frigid ice caps of the North and South Pole. He vowed to retrace the route of Marco Polo and to submerge to the great depths of the sea in a submarine. Goddard also wanted to study medicine, read the Bible cover to cover, all the works of Plato, Aristotle, William Shakespeare, Charles Dickens, the Encyclopedia Britannica in its entirety, and dozens of other great classic writings. He also had a vision of playing the violin and the flute, being married and raising a family.

At age forty-seven John Goddard had accomplished 103 of his 127 goals.

If one advances confidently in the direction of his dreams, and endeavors to live the life which he has imagined, he will meet with a success unexpected in common hours.

-HENRY DAVID THOREAU

The famous fitness icon, Jack LaLanne is a strong believer in the power of goals. Jack has set and accomplished goals as a way of life, making him one of the most profound examples in the fitness world today. LaLanne was once quoted in saying, "Anything in life is possible if you want it badly enough. I keep making new challenges and goals for myself, that's what keeps me going. With proper diet, exercise and attitude, you can live life to the fullest." Jack, at age forty-two set the world record of 1,033 push-ups in twenty-three minutes. He hasn't been sick since 1936, and celebrated his 70th birthday by swimming a full mile in the Long Beach Harbor with both his hands and feet tied, towing seventy boats behind him with his party guests on board. Now that's a Winning Mind Set!

One of the most essential things you need to do for yourself is to choose a goal that is important to you. Perfection does not exist –you can always do better and you can always grow.

-LES BROWN

The building block exercises for success

Now that you have all the information necessary to understand the importance and methodology of setting objectives in your life, let's get started. One of the best ways to begin with goal setting as a habit is to work from a list on a daily basis. Here are a few tips on using a list to increase your productivity and develop your goal setting muscles.

1) Work from a list every day. Update your list for the next day the night before or first thing the morning of. Write it down! Something amazing will happen when you materialize your thoughts on to paper.

2) Hold fast to your "standard procedure" of working from your list, refusing to do anything that is not on the list. This is accomplished by updating your list as you work through your day.

3) Evaluate tasks by deadline. Whenever possible work on your largest or most difficult, least favorite task first. This will ensure it gets done, not ending up on the next day's list. If you insist on completing the smaller tasks first you will make little headway. Small tasks will continue to appear as your day unfolds.

4) Evaluate each of your tasks for value and return. Which task will bring you the most return on your effort? One whale is worth a thousand buckets of minnows!

5) By working from a list everyday you will accomplish more in a week than most people do in months or even years.

6) Really, there is no such thing as unreasonable goals, just unreasonable time frames.

Where ever you are, begin now!

Winning Mind Set™ Exercises for Setting Objectives

Make a Map

An excellent way to approach your goals or challenge is by making a Project Map. Draw a circle in the center of a piece of paper and write your objective in the center at the top. Draw a line or arterial that leads you to another circle with the most important thing(s) you must do first in order to accomplish your objective. Repeat this for each of the tasks you will need to do to progress and accomplish your goal. Off these secondary circles draw another line to connect to a third circle indicating the ways or subcategories necessary to bring you to your success. We have used countless numbers of these maps to help us solve problems, overcome challenges and achieve our goals time and time again with exponential results.

Mind Storming

Another incredible key to overcoming tasks that may seem unachievable is called Mind Storming. Mind Storming is a method of problem solving using the concept of focusing on the solution rather than on the problem. First write the problem at the top of the page, next write down at least 20 solutions for your problem. Stay fixed on your goal of 20 solutions. At first it will seem very challenging, but as you search your mind, you squeeze out the one or more answers that will create the inner genius and insight that will find the best solution for any problem, and direct you in the successful achievement of any goal or objective, by using this method.

Mind Storming your Challenge

My Challenge:

1

2

3

4

5

6

7

8

9

10

11

12

13

14

15

16

17

18

19

20

Did you complete the exercise? Even if you think # 14 is the best possible solution, complete the entire 20. This cuts off most possibilities for addressing the problem from a conclusion.

7 VALUABLE KEY POINTS TO GOAL SETTING

1) Decide exactly what you want, be complete and specific.

2) Write it down clearly and in complete detail.

3) Set a deadline and several sub-deadlines that may be imperative toward the accomplishment of your objective. Keep to your timeline as best you can.

4) Next, make a plan of absolutely everything you need to do to achieve your goal. Once again, be as complete and detailed as possible.

5) Now, organize your list of activities in terms of time and priority, what's first, what's most important, what do you need to do before you can do something else, what needs to be done before anything else.

6) Take action toward your goal; begin now, do something to move you in the direction of your goal. This step is crucial; it is your first action step. It is that first step that creates the foundation for your future success.

7) Direct 100% total commitment toward the accomplishment of your goal. Don't give up!

Flexibility is absolute. If what you're doing isn't working, try changing your approach, if that doesn't work, change your approach again until you succeed.

Winning Mind Set™ Exercises – Setting Objectives

For the purpose of this exercise let's focus on a major goal you would like to achieve from any of the list in the beginning of the chapter.

Decide what you want. This is the most important step, if you don't know exactly what you want in complete detail you'll never get it! Write it down clearly and in complete detail.

Make an "Action Plan" of everything you need to do to get you closer to your goal.

Now, organize your "Action Plan" list in terms of activities pertaining to time and priority. What's first, what's most important?

Next set a deadline and several sub-deadlines for each action.

Take action toward your goal and begin immediately to do something to move you in the direction of your goal. What are you committed to do to take your first step forward?

Remember to direct 100% total commitment toward the accomplishment of your goal. Flexibility is absolute. If what you're doing isn't working, change your approach, if that doesn't work, change your approach again until you succeed. Every person who has achieved greatness has failed over and over to finally succeed.

Objectives
Key Points to Remember

1) Put yourself in the top 3% of all North Americans by having clear, written goals.

2) When you have determined your objective be sure to use the SMARTER method of progress. Be sure your goals are:

Specific
Measurable
Achievable
Realistic
Time-bound
Emotionally Satisfying
Relevant

3) Our goals support our values and our values in turn support us in the direction of our goals.

4) Work from a list every day, updating your list as you work through your day. Evaluate tasks by deadline. Whenever possible work on your largest or most difficult, least favorite task first. Evaluate each of your tasks for value and return. Which task will bring you the most return on your effort?

5) Use map out and mind-storming your challenges to aid in your success.

6) Goals help us to take control of the direction of change in a positive and empowering way. Your goals assure you that the changes you make in your life are in the direction you want to go.

7) Be sure to always have a list of numerous goals throughout your life. You will accomplish more in your lifetime than you ever thought possible.

I've missed more than nine thousand shots in my career. I've lost almost three hundred games. Twenty-six times I've been trusted to take the game-winning shot and missed. I've failed over and over in my life. That is why I succeed.

—MICHAEL JORDAN

Chapter Nine

Reinforcement

Hold yourself responsible for a higher standard
than anybody else expects of you.

-HENRY WARD BEECHER

People have an unbelievable capacity to change, develop, grow and evolve. Science has proven this: the brain, once thought to be fixed past a certain age, is now referred to as "plastic" given its ability to re-generate and develop over time.

The issue is not one of whether we can change, then, because with the right mindset people can absolutely change. Rather, the question is how to keep the positive changes that we make over time.

As far as reinforcing others, there is a lot of guidance available as to how to do that most effectively, tips such as:

- reinforce as close to the behavior as possible
- be specific in your reinforcement
- vary your schedule of reinforcement
- be positive in your reinforcement
- end on a positive note

It would be great if we all had people surrounding us who could do that for us. The reality is that most of us don't, so we need to rely on methods of self-reinforcement in addition to anything we can get from others. To help you in reinforcing the positive changes in

267

your life, then, let us share with you the following The Winning Mind Set™ tools for reinforcing new behaviors.

Five Keys to Effective Reinforcement

1. **Focus on one thing at a time**
2. **Praise Progress, not perfection**
3. **Harness the power of Anchors**
4. **Utilize the power of reminders**
5. **Establish a "support structure"**

Focus on one thing at a time

Tom Landry, who at the time the coach of the Super Bowl Champion Dallas Cowboys, was asked, "In all your years of coaching, what is the most important thing you have learned about developing new skills?" Landry replied, "Focus on one thing at a time."

It is difficult for us to work on more than one significant change at a time. Out of our enthusiasm it may be tempting for us to work on many things at once, though it generally does not meet with success. Rather, it is more effective to focus down on one particular behavior and work on that until it has reached the desired level of proficiency.

To do this, you can ask: What is the one thing that will make the biggest difference in my _____ (career, performance, results, relationships, health, etc.)?

Seeing progress in a certain area is fulfilling and self-reinforcing. Once you see some progress in one area and are satisfied that your new habits and behaviors are consistent, you can move to another area, revisiting as often as needed.

Praise progress, not perfection

Dan Inosanto is one of the most gifted martial artists in the world. He is probably best known to the general public for his long-time friendship with Bruce Lee. In fact, he was the man personally chosen by Bruce Lee to continue teaching his style of martial arts. Dan once told to us that it takes about 1,000 repetitions of a physical movement before it becomes embedded in your nervous system, or what is known as "muscle memory." That seems like a lot of repetitions, doesn't it? 1,000? He said that the secret to mastering a technique is not so much of trying to get it down to less than 1,000, but rather to control your emotions so that you don't get upset when you haven't got it perfect after the third try.

Just as it is important to set bite-size goals, it is equally important to reinforce your progress all along the way, to praise progress and not perfection. Take the example of a small child learning to draw. If a little kid shows you a scribbled drawing and asks how you like her cat, you aren't going to say, "What is this? This is terrible! It doesn't look anything like a cat." No, you will reinforce her for where she is at the time. "Wow, honey, that's a great cat. Look at all the colors!"

That way, she feels encouraged to continue to practice so that she can get better, so she can do the 1,000 repetitions that Dan Inosanto described. While it may seem odd to praise yourself, it is an important step in helping you to reinforce where you are and what you need to do to get to the next step. Examples include:

- One thing I did well today was …
- I improved in this area by …
- I learned …
- I learned what not to do in …
- What is great about this is …
- I think I could make more progress if I …

We covered this in the use of questions in the Emotions chapter. As simple as this technique is, it is also very powerful. Make sure you frame your statements in the positive. It's the same thing if you say to a child, "Don't *spill your milk*", he has to picture spilling the milk to understand the negation of that action. Instead, "Keep your milk in your cup while you drink it," is a much better choice, since that is actually what you want him to do. This method of communication is also solution oriented, not problem based as you are actually conveying the solution to the individual, not the problem in reference to what you "Don't Want." This is the same principle you want to use when reinforcing a behavior choice in yourself. Tell yourself what you want or need to do, as opposed to what you don't want or shouldn't do. This directs you where you want to go, and not where you don't.

Harness the power of anchors

Recall that in the Associations chapter, you learned how to set an anchor. Anchors are very powerful tools for helping to reinforce a positive outlook. You may be in a situation where you are not doing well in a meeting at work, during a sales call, or an athletic event, on the edge of losing your temper. It is tempting to go down that path of frustration, despair, overwhelm, etc. – to run that pattern. You can interrupt that pattern by firing off a positive anchor – one for confidence, patience, curiosity, or which ever emotional state will best help you deal effectively with the situation.

Utilize the power of reminders

There are other steps you can take to remind you of your goals such as:

- Taping your goals up on the bathroom mirror or some place where you will see it every day. Your mind is

most receptive to information in the periods when
you wake up and before you go to sleep

- Get images of your goals if possible, pictures can be more motivating than words.

- Put up pictures of role models. Many people wear the WWJD bracelets to remind them of how they want to treat other people.

- Utilize acronyms. The power of BEHAVIOR™ is that it is a simple way to categorize a lot of information. If we didn't use this, it would be pretty difficult to remember the gamut of tools and techniques. But with the acronym, it makes it fairly straightforward. Use this as a reference by asking, "What are my core **B**eliefs and have they changed? How are my **E**motions affecting my outcome? What **H**abits have I developed, fallen back into, etc.?" Follow through with pertinent questions for each letter/area of the BEHAVIOR acronym and ask yourself what areas are affecting your success or failure at this point in time.

One person we worked with used the acronym SELL for his values. Serve, Encourage, Learn and Love. He said, like in selling, if you don't take action, you're not accomplishing anything. He used a visual image – a logo if you will – to help motivate and remind him to take action in those areas that meant the most to him.

- Keep a journal. We all slide away from our focal point from time to time and need to adjust back on track. Your journal entries can become a great source of reference, provide insight into how far you have come, and reinforce what you have accomplished.

- Create a Values and Goals wheel, where your most important value is in the center, and your other values are surrounding it. Within each values space you can list out specific goals.

Establish a "support structure"

> *...don't try to change yourself,*
> *change your environment.*
>
> -B.F. SKINNER

The power of a support structure is amazing. Whether that takes the form of a mastermind group, a training partner, a coach, a support group, a trusted friend, a mentor, or an elder, their role can be incredibly effective in helping you achieve the kind of personal success you desire. These people are there for you to coach, nudge, cajole, tease, and hold you accountable for your actions. They can give you a hug or kick you in the butt, depending on the need.

To properly engage a support structure, you will first need a person or people who absolutely believe in your potential. It doesn't mean that they won't challenge you or force you to think through your plans, but they need to be a strong supporter in your potential to achieve your goals.

Secondly, you need to have a support structure consistent with your goals. If you want to be a world-class athlete and your coach has never produced a world-class champion, he or she may not be the best choice. If you aspire to a certain position in a company, you need to associate with people who have first-hand knowledge of what it takes to succeed in such an environment. You want to surround yourself with people who have experience at the level you want to be.

Thirdly, you need to be honest and up front about what you want to achieve and what role you want them to play with respect to frequency, directness, and detail.

Reinforcement
Key Points To Remember

1) Focus on one thing at a time
2) Praise Progress, not perfection
3) Harness the power of Anchors
4) Utilize the power of reminders
   - Tape up your goals where you will see them every morning and night
   - Use visual images to inspire you
   - Utilize acronyms
   - Use role models or other motivating examples
   - Keep a journal
   - Create a Values / Goal wheel
5) Establish a "support structure"

Man's mind stretched to a new idea
never goes back to its original dimensions.

-OLIVER WENDELL HOLMES

Chapter Ten

Your Challenge

Life is not about finding yourself.
Life is about creating yourself.

Well, you've done it! You have made it all the way here. You have committed a lot of time and energy studying what it takes to have a Winning Mind Set™. You have dedicated your efforts to make some remarkable improvements within yourself.

There is an abundance of material in this book, and we hope you don't expect yourself to master it all overnight. There is certainly no need to. We hope you will use this book as a reference guide as you progress in your life successes.

Imagine, what if all you did is utilize the power of references to help yourself empower your beliefs, what might happen? Think of the changes that might occur if all you did was realize the incredible power of something as simple as a question, breathing, reframing, or a metaphor, to change the way you feel? Or if all you did was understand how to interrupt your or someone's pattern, and use an anchor to help get into a resourceful state? What would happen if all you did was take the opportunity to get in touch with your value system, and understand how to determine your own rules in your game? Picture in your mind the possibilities, if all you did was understand the power an identity has on impacting behavior, and applied that to your life right now? What if all you did was use and share with others a SMARTER way to set objectives? What if you were to use what you learned to more effectively utilize more of your amazing potential? Just imagine the difference if all you did, after you've read this material, is get a better sense of what motivates yourself and other people, and how to better communicate, interact and build rapport?

Hopefully you are walking away with some ideas that can help you become more of who you are and maybe even assisting others in doing the same. Perhaps we will meet someday and you can tell us about your successes, or perhaps you can write to us. In either case, we hope that in some way we have been able to assist you in making some improvements in your life. We admire and respect you for never settling for anything less than you can be.

There can be no happiness if the things we believe in are different from the things we do.

-FREYA STARK

Bibliography

An Unused Intelligence: Physical Thinking for 21ˢᵗ Century Leadership, by Andy Bryner and Dawna Markova, Ph. D. Conari Press, Berkeley, CA., 1996.

Awaken the Giant Within: How to take immediate control of your mental, emotional, physical and financial destiny!, by Anthony Robbins. Summit Books, New York, 1991.

Beyond Success: The 15 Secrets of a Winning Life!, by Brian D. Biro. Pygmalion Press, Hamilton, Montana, 1995.

Breathwalk: Breathing Your Way to a Revitalized Body, Mind, and Spirit, by Gurucharan Singh Khalsa, Ph.D., and Yogi Bhajan, Ph. D. Broadway Books, New York, 2000.

Don't Shoot the Dog! How to Improve Yourself and Others Through Behavioral Training, by Karen Pryor. Simon and Schuster, New York. 1984.

Healing in Hypnosis: The Seminars, Workshops and Lectures of Milton H. Erickson, Volume I, edited by Ernest L. Rossi, Margaret O. Ryan and Florence A. Sharp. Irvington Publishers, Inc. New York, 1983.

Hypnosis for Change, by Josie Hadley and Carol Staudacher. New Harbinger Publications, Oakland, CA, 1996.

Hypnotherapy Scripts: A Neo-Ericksonian Approach to Persuasive Healing, by Ronald A. Havens, and Catherine Walters. Brunner / Mazel Publishers, New York, 1989.

Lessons from the Masters: Seven Keys to Peak Performance and Inner Peace, by Jim Brault. Center Line Press, Rochester, NY, 1998.

Life Reframing in Hypnosis: The Seminars, Workshops and Lectures of Milton H. Erickson, Volume II, edited by Ernest L. Rossi and Margaret O. Ryan. Irvington Publishers, Inc. New York, 1985.

Mind-Body Communication in Hypnosis: The Seminars, Workshops and Lectures of Milton H. Erickson, Volume III, edited by Ernest L. Rossi and Margaret O. Ryan. Irvington Publishers, Inc. New York, 1986.

My Voice Will Go With You: The Teaching Tales of Milton H. Erickson, M.D., edited and with commentary by Sidney Rosen, M.D. WW Norton & Co., New York, 1982.

Patterns of the Hypnotic Techniques of Milton H. Erickson, M.D., Volume 1, by Richard Bandler and John Grinder. Meta Publications, Capitola, California, 1975.

Think Like A Winner, Dr. Walter Doyle Staples Pelican Publishing Co., Gretna, Louisiana, 1991.

Your Performing Edge, Dr. JoAnn Dahlkoetter Pulgas Ridge Press, San Carlos, California, 2001.

The Psychology of Success, Brian Tracy Nightingale-Conant Co. Niles, Illinois.

The Mental Edge, Kenneth Baum The Berkley Publishing Group, New York, New York, 1999.

The Power of Focus, Jack Canfield, Mark Victor Hansen and Les Hewitt Health Communications, Inc. Deerfield Beach, Florida, 2000.

Webster's New Collegiate Dictionary, G. & C. Merriam Company, Springfield, Massachusetts, 1973.

About the Authors

Jim Brault

Since 1978, Jim Brault has sought out and shared methods for realizing more of ones' potential. His work has led him to study a variety of disciplines, including clinical, developmental, physiological and behavioral psychology, meditation, yoga, a number of internal and external martial arts, Neuro-Associative Conditioning ™, Neuro-Linguistic Programming ™, Qigong, Hypnotherapy, Organizational Development, Organizational Behavior, Team Performance, Coaching, and Leadership Development. Jim holds a Bachelor's degree in Psychology from Binghamton University, and a Master's Degree in Industrial and Labor Relations from Cornell University. After a successful high school and college wrestling career, Jim began his study of martial arts in 1983. He earned a second-degree black belt in Tae Kwon Do, and is a certified instructor in Wing Chun Kung Fu.

For four years he owned and operated a franchise of peak performance coach Anthony Robbins, helping thousands of people through the personal development and sales training programs. Jim is a certified instructor in Kundalini Yoga and meditation, the author of *Lessons from the Masters: Seven Keys to Peak Performance and Inner Peace,* and at age 44 began competing in the sport of Powerlifting. He currently is a Director of Human Resources for Eastman Kodak, and lives with his wife and three children in Rochester, NY.

Kevin Seaman

Kevin Seaman has taught as a course instructor in the Physical Education Department at Cornell since 1993, where he has taught a credit course titled The Winning Mind Set since 2002. Kevin has written dozens of articles featured in National and International Magazines. He is currently on the writing staff of contributors for Bodybuilding.com, the largest website for Professional and amateur bodybuilders in the United States.

Kevin is a guest lecturer and workshop presenter for numerous business, educational, sports and recreational organizations including the Johnson School of Business MBA Fellowship at Cornell University.

Kevin began his martial arts training in 1970 in Southern California. To date he has achieved advanced instructor levels in seven different martial arts systems and is a certified boxing coach, certified police defensive tactics instructor, and published author. In addition to this, his study and application of the art and science of personal achievement, mental fitness and performance coaching has spanned over two decades, and he has read over 200 books on the subject. He has taught the martial arts helping to empower thousands of students of all ages on both an academic and vocational level for over 30 years.

Kevin has extensive experience in the education and coaching of amateur and professional competitors in Thai boxing, kickboxing, boxing, shootwrestling, NHB and full contact stickfighting. He has had a positive influence on the athletic careers of thousands of athletes, including high school and collegiate athletes, Golden Gloves State Champions, Empire Games medalists, national champions, All Americans, and international champions, as well as dozens of

Professional Athletes.

Kevin is a three-time Hall of Fame inductee, being inducted into the ZDK, AMA and World Martial Arts Hall of Fame's. In 2001, he was honored for a Diamond Lifetime Achievement Award in Atlantic City, at the largest Black Tie event of it's kind ever, in the history of the martial arts.

Kevin has competed in the martial arts on a regional, national, and international level for over a decade, and was an "Eastern National Champion" in both floor forms and full contact competition. At the age of 37, Mr. Seaman was a World Champion Silver Medalist in full contact stickfighting competing in Southeast Asia at the 1992 World, Kali, Arnis Championships at the Aquino Memorial Stadium in Manila, Philippines.